Exit Strategies for Covered Call Writing and Selling Cash-Secured Puts

How to enter, manage and calculate trade adjustments for all market conditions

By Dr. Alan Ellman: President of
The Blue Collar Investor Corp.

Trade Management Calculator developed by
Dr. Alan Ellman
and Barry Bergman, BCI Managing Director

Exit Strategies for Covered Call Writing and Selling Cash-Secured Puts

 First Printing: December

ISBN: 978-1-956793-28-4

Printed in the United States of America

Published by Digital Publishing of Florida, Inc.
www.digitaldata-corp.com

Dedication

This book is dedicated to you, the BCI community. You are the folks who put us on the financial map. Your support and loyalty over many years have provided us with the ideas that have allowed us to produce hundreds of articles and videos along with our best-selling books, calculators and watchlists. These have allowed us to reach tens of thousands of investors all over the world. We could not have done this without you.

This book is dedicated to you, our extended family, who have elevated BCI to heights we never dreamed possible. Thank you!

Table of Contents

Acknowledgments

I would like to acknowledge and offer my gratitude to the incredible BCI team.

Barry Bergman, BCI Managing Director, and I have been working together for almost 15 years. We worked on the *Trade Management Calculator and Exit Management System* for over a year and created a product that is the only one of its kind anywhere. His knowledge of Excel was critical to the creation of this unique product.

Barbara, Darius, Gabe, Adele, Adam and Linda are also indispensable members of the BCI team. I am so lucky to have the opportunity to be part of such a talented organization. I consider this book to be a team effort.

Introduction

In the 1990s, when I started studying option-selling strategies, there was a huge gap in the information available to maximize trading results. How do we manage our trades after entering our covered call writing or put-selling positions? I sensed that there were significant opportunities inherent in these strategies but realized that there was a lot of work that needed to be done to create a system that will allow us to substantially beat the market on a consistent basis.

Each time I executed a trade, I would analyze it after-the-fact. How could I have mitigated those losses? How could I have enhanced those gains? Could I have converted those losses into gains? I always had a bit of a knack for math and so I started developing various formulas, rules and guidelines to adjust these trades in order to accomplish the goal of achieving the highest possible return levels given the condition that a specific trade was in.

I understood that when we are investing in the stock market, there is inherent risk. Whenever we seek to achieve higher than a risk-free return (Treasuries, for example), we, by definition, are undertaking risk. We need to manage and mitigate this exposure. Risk management is the ultimate goal and focus of this book.

Exit Strategies for Covered Call Writing and Selling Cash-Secured Puts is divided into 2 sections. The first is dedicated to covered call writing and the second to selling cash-secured puts. Each section will list all the exit strategy opportunities available, define the terms and explain when to implement each strategy. Then a real-life example is given where initial trade entries, initial trade returns, trade adjustment entries and final calculations are displayed.

The actual entries and calculations are displayed using the *BCI Trade Management Calculator (TMC),* a one-of-a-kind tool that acts as a trading log. While you can do the calculations described in the book manually, in my humble opinion, if we can see the step-by-step trade entries, adjustments and calculations in a single spreadsheet, we can better understand the mechanics of our trades. This will allow us to elevate our success to the highest possible levels. Simply stated, it will make us more accomplished investors.

I envision this book sitting on our desk adjacent to our computers. When a trade turns against us or turns out far better than anticipated, we can turn to the specific example in the book and subsequently apply that position management opportunity to our portfolios. After a few months, these concepts will become second nature and we'll be able to put the book back into our bookcase but it will always be there, if needed.

Several of the real-life examples were tweaked to accommodate other exit strategy opportunities. The execution of the initial trades, in these instances, were the same, but I included the start-to-finish images for a specific reason. After reading this book one or more times, we can then use it as a reference book. This is why I felt it important to show all strategies from initial entry to final results at the expense of some minor redundancy. *Whether you use the BCI Trade*

Management Calculator or another trading log, the information will allow us to trade in a non-emotional manner by being prepared for every possible positive or negative event.

Exit strategies and trade adjustments are critical to maximizing the success of our trades. My objectives, when writing this book, were to give investors the tools to manage their trades and maximize the positive outcomes we all seek. Only you can determine if I have been successful in achieving these goals.

Section I: Exit Strategies for Covered Call Writing

Chapter 1

What is Covered Call Writing?

Introduction

Covered call writing is a low-risk investment strategy that combines two different strategies:

- Stock ownership
- **Selling** options

Most retail investors are familiar with buying and selling shares of stock but a low percentage trades stock options.

Let's first define the three words in the strategy name:

Covered means we first buy the stock before selling the option. We know our cost-basis, the cost of the stock. This protects us from catastrophic capital loss. As a matter of fact, the word *protected* can be substituted for the word *covered*. **This does not imply that there is no risk in the strategy but rather, it is a low-risk strategy.**

Call is the type of option we are selling. The option buyer (also called the option holder) is given the right, but not the obligation, to buy our shares at a price that we determine (the strike price), by a date that we determine (the expiration date). In return for undertaking this obligation, we receive a cash premium that is dictated by the market. Stated differently, *option buyers have rights and option sellers have obligations.*

Writing means that we are *selling* the option, not buying it. It is the initial sale of the option (noted as *sell-to-open* or STO on our trade execution forms).

To sum up: we buy a stock and sell an option which gives the buyer (option holder) the right, but not the obligation, to buy our shares at a certain price (called the *strike price*) by a certain date (known as the *expiration date*). In return for undertaking this contractual obligation we receive a cash premium that is determined by the market.

Preview example

In this hypothetical, we will buy 100 shares of BCI Corp. at $28.00 per-share for a total investment of $2800.00 (commissions not included but we should be using online discount brokers to minimize trading costs). It is important to note that each options contract represents 100 shares of the underlying security.

Now that we own the shares (we are *covered*), we are free to sell the option. We then select a sales price (also called the option *strike price*) of $30.00 (as one example) and select a 1-month expiration date (my personal preference in most, but not in all, of my portfolios). A typical return for this option sale could be $1.00 per share or $100.00 for the contract (called the *option premium* or *call value*). This represents an initial 3.6%, 1-month return based on a cost basis of $2800.00. The *implied volatility (IV)* of the underlying security is directly related to the premium return. Securities with higher IVs will have larger premiums and vice-versa.

At the end of the contract month (most monthly options expire on the third Friday of the month at 4 PM ET), the option holder will decide whether to exercise the option and buy our shares. If the price is below $30.00, the agreed upon sales price, the option will expire worthless and will not be *exercised* as our shares will remain in our portfolio. Now, we are free to sell another option on those same shares in the following contract month (different from calendar month). Our 1-month realized option profit is 3.6% ($1.00/ $28.00), in this hypothetical.

If the price of the stock is above $30.00 as the contract is expiring, the option will be exercised (unless we buy back the option prior to expiration to avoid exercise) and our shares sold at $30.00 per-share. In this scenario, we generate an additional $2.00 per- share profit or $200.00 for the 100 shares. Our total profit becomes $300.00, $200.00 from the sale of the stock and $100.00 from the sale of the option. This represents a 10.7%, 1-month realized return.

Now, **there is some risk in this strategy.** The risk is in the stock, not in the sale of the option. If share value declines by more than the option premium received, we can start to lose money. This is why we must have a series of exit strategies and adjustments in place to mitigate losses or turn losses into gains.

Position management is one of the three required skills for covered call writing and is the focal point of this book. The other two are stock selection and option selection. Mastering stock and option selection techniques is detailed in both versions of *The Complete Encyclopedia for Covered Call Writing* (classic edition should be read first).

Summary

Covered call writing is a conservative, low-risk, cash-generating strategy that combines stock ownership and option selling. *Stock selection, option selection and position management are the necessary and critical skills needed to achieve maximum success.* We will now move on to the exit strategy opportunities available to us after entering our covered call writing trades.

Chapter 2

Allowing Exercise

What is allowing exercise?

When our covered call options are expiring in-the-money (with intrinsic-value), we can buy back the short call to prevent exercise and retain the underlying shares, or take no action and *allow our shares to be sold* (or exercised) at the call strike price. By allowing exercise, we will have maximized our option returns and will have a realized share capital gain (if an OTM call was sold) or breakeven (if an ITM call was sold when factoring in the intrinsic-value component of the option premium). To highlight this strategy, we will use a real-life example with Energy Select Sector SPDR Fund (NYSE: XLE).

When to consider allowing exercise

We use this strategy approach when the original call strike is expiring ITM and we do not plan to use this security in the upcoming contract cycle. For example, if there is an upcoming earnings report in the next contract expiration period, we would allow exercise. Another reason to consider allowing exercise would be if the rolling calculations did not align with our stated initial time-value return goal range.

Real-life example with XLE

- 1/24/2022: Buy 100 x XLE at $60.30
- 1/24/22: STO 1 x 2/18/2022 $62.50 (OTM) call at $1.78
- 2/18/2022: XLE trading at $67.93 leaving the $62.50 strike deep ITM
- 2/18/2022: Take no action and allow the option to exercise and shares are sold at $62.50

Initial trade entries

Stock Symbol	Industry	Entry Trade Date	ER Date	Ex-Div Date	Entry Trade Expiry Date	Entry Stock Price [$/sh]	Entry Call Strike Price [$]	Entry Call Option Premium [$/sh]	Number Of Shares [#]
XLE	Energy	01/24/22	NA	03/20/22	02/18/22	$ 60.30	$ 62.50	$ 1.78	100

Figure 1: XLE: Entering Our Initial Trade

Initial trade returns

OPENING TRADE						
Expected # Of Days In Trade [#]	Time-Value Per-Share [$/sh]	Intrinsic-Value Per-Share [$/sh]	Upside Value Per-Share [$/sh]	Breakeven Value Per-Share [$/sh]	Return On Option ROO [%]	Return On Option ROO Annual'zd [%]
26	$ 1.78	$ -	$ 2.20	$ 58.52	2.95%	41.44%

Upside Potential [%]	Downside Protect. [%]	Trade ROO Premium [$]	Trade Upside Premium [$]	Total Capital Invested [$]
3.65%	0.00%	$ 178.00	$ 220.00	$ 6,030.00

Figure 2: XLE: Initial Trade Returns

The spreadsheet shows an initial time-value return of 2.95% (brown cell), 41.44% annualized based on a 26-day trade with 3.65% upside potential (green cell), resulting in a 26-day maximum return of 6.60%. The breakeven price point is $58.52 (yellow cell).

How to manage these situations

Since the strike is ITM as expiration approaches, the initial option trade return is maximized. The shares are worth $62.50, our contract obligation to sell price. We enter the final stock value as the current value at expiration as we decide to allow exercise and accept our shares being sold at the $62.50 strike. We, then, check the final stock and option realized returns.

Trade adjustment entries

Stock Symbol	Exit Strategy Selected	Adjust. Trade Date	Adjust. Expiry Date	BTC Entry Option Price [$/Sh]	STO Entry #2 Strike Price [$]	STO Entry #2 Option Premium [$/Sh]	Final Stock Sale Price If Sold [$/Sh]	Final Unsold Stock Price [$/Sh]
XLE	Allow Exercise	02/18/22					$ 62.50	

Figure 3: XLE: Allowing Exercise Adjustments

Shares are valued at $62.50, the ITM strike price, at expiration.

Final calculations

Final Net Option Profit/Loss [$/Sh]	Final Net Option Profit/Loss [$]	Final Net Option Return [%]	Realized Final Stock Profit/Loss per share [$/Sh]	Realized Final $ Total Stock Profit/Loss [$]	Realized Final Stock Profit/Loss [%]	Unrealized Final Stock Profit/Loss [$/Sh]	Unrealized Final Stock $ Total Stock Profit/Loss [$]	Unreal. Final Stock % Total Stock Profit/Loss [%]
$ 1.78	$ 178.00	2.95%	$ 2.20	$ 220.00	3.65%	$ -	$ -	

FINAL RESULT	
Combined Final Trade Total Profit/Loss [$]	Combined Final Trade Total Profit/Loss [%]
$ 398.00	6.60%

Figure 4: XLE: Final Results After Allowing Exercise

The spreadsheet shows a final net option return of 2.95% with a realized final stock appreciation of 3.65%. This resulted in a gain of $398.00 per-contract or 6.60% for the 26-day period. The cash created by the sale of XLE can be used to establish another covered call position the Monday after expiration Friday.

Discussion

We normally allow exercise of our options when the strike is expiring in-the-money at expiration. This is based on a decision that we do not plan to use this underlying in the next contract cycle which is determined by our system screening and calculation requirements.

Chapter 3

Buy Back Option/Keeping Stock

What is buying back the option and keeping the stock?

There are situations where we may want to close the short call and take no action through contract expiration. The main reason is typically because premium value has declined due to *Theta* (time-value or time-decay erosion) and a nice option profit can be realized without retaining the contract obligation. We will use the XLE example from Chapter 2 to explain how this exit strategy is executed.

When to consider buying back the option and retaining the stock

If share value has remained in a narrow range during the current contract and *Delta* (price change in the underlying security, see glossary for more information) is playing only a minor role in the premium change while Theta (see glossary for more information) is eroding premium value, we may want to realize our profits. This will allow for potential share appreciation without being capped by the strike ceiling as we wait for the start of the next contract cycle.

Real-life example with XLE

- 1/24/2022: Buy 100 x XLE at $60.30
- 1/24/22: STO 1 x 2/18/2022 $62.50 (OTM) call at $1.78
- 2/9/2022: XLE trading at $60.93 leaving the $62.50 strike still slightly OTM
- 2/9/2022: BTC the $62.50 call strike at $0.35

Initial trade entries

Stock Symbol	Industry	Entry Trade Date	ER Date	Ex-Div Date	Entry Trade Expiry Date	Entry Stock Price [$/sh]	Entry Call Strike Price [$]	Entry Call Option Premium [$/sh]	Number Of Shares [#]
XLE	Energy	01/24/22	NA	03/20/22	02/18/22	$ 60.30	$ 62.50	$ 1.78	100

Figure 5: XLE: Entering Our Initial Trade

Initial trade returns

OPENING TRADE						
Expected # Of Days In Trade [#]	Time-Value Per-Share [$/sh]	Intrinsic-Value Per-Share [$/sh]	Upside Value Per-Share [$/sh]	Breakeven Value Per-Share [$/sh]	Return On Option ROO [%]	Return On Option ROO Annual'zd [%]
26	$ 1.78	$ -	$ 2.20	$ 58.52	2.95%	41.44%

Upside Potential [%]	Downside Protect. [%]	Trade ROO Premium [$]	Trade Upside Premium [$]	Total Capital Invested [$]
3.65%	0.00%	$ 178.00	$ 220.00	$ 6,030.00

Figure 6: XLE: Initial Trade Returns

The spreadsheet shows an initial time-value return of 2.95% (brown cell), 41.44% annualized based on a 26-day trade with 3.65% upside potential (green cell), resulting in a 26-day maximum return of 6.60%. The breakeven price point is $58.52 (yellow cell).

How to manage these situations

We enter the date the short call is closed, the BTC price and the current market price of the shares to assess the current trade status.

Trade adjustment entries

Stock Symbol	Exit Strategy Selected	Adjust. Trade Date	Adjust. Expiry Date	BTC Entry Option Price [$/Sh]	STO Entry #2 Strike Price [$]	STO Entry #2 Option Premium [$/Sh]	Final Stock Sale Price If Sold [$/Sh]	Final Unsold Stock Price [$/Sh]
XLE	Buy Back Option/Keep Stock	02/09/22		$ 0.35				$ 60.93

Figure 7: XLE: Buying Back Option/ Keeping Stock Adjustments

Shares are valued at $60.93 at the time of the trade adjustment.

Final calculations

Final Net Option Profit/Loss [$/Sh]	Final Net Option Profit/Loss [$]	Final Net Option Return [%]	Realized Final Stock Profit/Loss per share [$/Sh]	Realized Final $ Total Stock Profit/Loss [$]	Realized Final Stock Profit/Loss [%]	Unrealized Final Stock Profit/Loss [$/Sh]	Unrealized Final Stock $ Total Stock Profit/Loss [$]	Unreal. Final Stock % Total Stock Profit/Loss [%]
$ 1.43	$ 143.00	2.37%	$ -	$ -	-	$ 0.63	$ 63.00	1.04%

FINAL RESULT	
Combined Final Trade Total Profit/Loss [$]	Combined Final Trade Total Profit/Loss [%]
$ 206.00	3.42%

Figure 8: XLE: Final Results After Closing the Short Call

The spreadsheet shows a final net option return of 2.37% with an unrealized current stock appreciation of 1.04%. This resulted in an unrealized gain of $206.00 per-contract or 3.42% for the current trade status.

Discussion

We consider buying back our call options when share price is trading in a narrow range and we can retain a large portion of the original option premium while eliminating our contract obligation. There may be other reasons we are motivated to close the short call and take no action but the reason presented is most typical.

Chapter 4

Expire Worthless

What is allowing our options to expire worthless?

When our covered call options are expiring out-of-the-money (with no intrinsic-value), there is no need to roll the option as shares will be retained in our portfolios after expiration of the contracts. By taking no action and allowing our options to expire worthless, we will have maximized our option returns and will have an unrealized (shares not sold) capital gain or loss on the stock side. To highlight this exit strategy choice, we will use a real-life example with United Therapeutics Corp., Inc. (Nasdaq: UTHR).

When to consider allowing options to expire worthless

When the original option strike price is expiring OTM and there is no need to mitigate losses, we take no action and retain the shares through expiration. We can then craft our plan for the next contract cycle over the weekend. This includes the decision to retain or sell the underlying shares for the next contract cycle.

Real-life example with UTHR

- 2/22/21: Buy 100 x UTHR at $155.90
- 2/22/21: STO 1 x 3/21/2021 $160.00 (OTM) call at $3.50
- 3/21/2021: UTHR trading at $158.25

- 3/21/2021: Take no action and allow the option to expire worthless

Initial trade entries

Stock Symbol	Industry	Entry Trade Date	ER Date	Ex-Div Date	Entry Trade Expiry Date	Entry Stock Price [$/sh]	Entry Call Strike Price [$]	Entry Call Option Premium [$/sh]	Number Of Shares [#]
UTHR	Healthcare	02/22/21	04/20/21	NA	03/21/21	$ 155.90	$ 160.00	$ 3.50	100

Figure 9: UTHR: Entering Our Initial Trade

Initial trade returns

OPENING TRADE						
Expected # Of Days In Trade [#]	Time-Value Per-Share [$/sh]	Intrinsic-Value Per-Share [$/sh]	Upside Value Per-Share [$/sh]	Breakeven Value Per-Share [$/sh]	Return On Option ROO [%]	Return On Option ROO Annual'zd [%]
28	$ 3.50	$ -	$ 4.10	$ 152.40	2.25%	29.27%

Upside Potential [%]	Downside Protect. [%]	Trade ROO Premium [$]	Trade Upside Premium [$]	Total Capital Invested [$]
2.63%	0.00%	$ 350.00	$ 410.00	$ 15,590.00

Figure 10: UTHR: Initial Trade Returns

The spreadsheet shows an initial time-value return of 2.25%, 29.27% annualized based on a 28-day trade with 2.63% upside potential, resulting in a 28-day maximum return of 4.88%. The breakeven price point is $152.40 (yellow cell).

How to manage these situations

Since the strike is OTM as expiration approaches, the initial option trade return is maximized. We enter the final unsold stock value as the current market value at expiration. We, then, check the final option realized and stock unrealized returns.

Trade adjustment entries

Stock Symbol	Exit Strategy Selected	Adjust. Trade Date	Adjust. Expiry Date	BTC Entry Option Price [$/Sh]	STO Entry #2 Strike Price [$]	STO Entry #2 Option Premium [$/Sh]	Final Stock Sale Price If Sold [$/Sh]	Final Unsold Stock Price [$/Sh]
UTHR	Expire Worthless	03/21/21						$ 158.25

Figure 11: UTHR: Expiring Worthless Adjustment

Shares are valued at $158.25 at expiration.

Final calculations

Final Net Option Profit/Loss [$/Sh]	Final Net Option Profit/Loss [$]	Final Net Option Return [%]	Realized Final Stock Profit/Loss per share [$/Sh]	Realized Final $ Total Stock Profit/Loss [$]	Realized Final Stock Profit/Loss [%]	Unrealized Final Stock Profit/Loss [$/Sh]	Unrealized Final Stock $ Total Stock Profit/Loss [$]	Unreal. Final Stock % Total Stock Profit/Loss [%]
$ 3.50	$ 350.00	2.25%	$ -	$ -	-	$ 2.35	$ 235.00	1.51%

FINAL RESULT	
Combined Final Trade Total Profit/Loss [$]	Combined Final Trade Total Profit/Loss [%]
$ 585.00	3.75%

Figure 12: UTHR: Final Results After Allowing Options to Expire Worthless

The spreadsheet shows a final net option return of 2.25% with an unrealized final stock appreciation of 1.51%. This resulted in a gain of $585.00 per-contract or 3.75% for the 28-day period.

Another covered call be written for the next contract cycle with a cost-basis of $158.25 or the shares can be sold after the market opens on Monday.

Discussion

We normally allow the options to expire worthless when the strike is expiring out-of-the-money at expiration. At the start of the next contract cycle, decisions are made as to whether we will retain or sell the underlying securities.

Chapter 5

Hitting a Double and Keeping the Stock

What is hitting a double?

Hitting a double involves buying back the short call using our 20%/10% guidelines (discussed in *The Complete Encyclopedias* and below) and then re-selling that same option when share price recovers. The *post-exit strategy chart will show a classic V-shaped pattern* where share price first declines and then recovers. This creates 2 income streams in the same contract period with the same underlying security and investment.

What are the 20%/10% Guidelines?

These are guidelines that assist us in determining when to buy back a short call if share price is declining. In the first 2 weeks of a 4-week contract, or in the first 3 weeks of a 5-week contract, we buy back the short call if the premium value declines to 20% of the original captured premium. This is accomplished by setting up a buy-to-close (BTC), good-until-cancelled (GTC) limit order immediately after entering our covered call writing position.

For example, if we sold an option for $2.00 per-share, we buy back the short call at $0.40 or less in the first half of a monthly contract. In the last 2 weeks of a monthly contract, we change that 20% BTC GTC limit order from 20% to 10%.

If the original option was sold for $2.00, the new limit order is set at $0.20 or less. This partially automates the exit strategy process. I make a note in my calendar prior to the last 2 weeks of a monthly contract to change all 20% BTC GTC limit orders to 10%.

When to consider hitting a double

We, generally, use this exit strategy in the first half of a monthly contract (there are exceptions and can be implemented later in a contract) when shares price declines and there is adequate time for share price recovery.

Real-life example with SPDR S&P Biotech ETF (NYSE: XBI)

- 2/26/2019: 100 shares XBI purchased at $90.25
- 2/26/2019 Sell-to-open 1 contract of the March 21, 2019 $92.00 calls at $1.50
- 3/6/2019: Buy-to-close the $92.00 call at $0.15 (10% guideline)
- 3/13/2019: Sell-to-open the $92.00 call at $0.55
- 3/21/2019: XBI price is $91.69 at expiration
- 3/21/2019: $92.00 calls expire worthless

XBI: Classic V-Shaped Chart Pattern

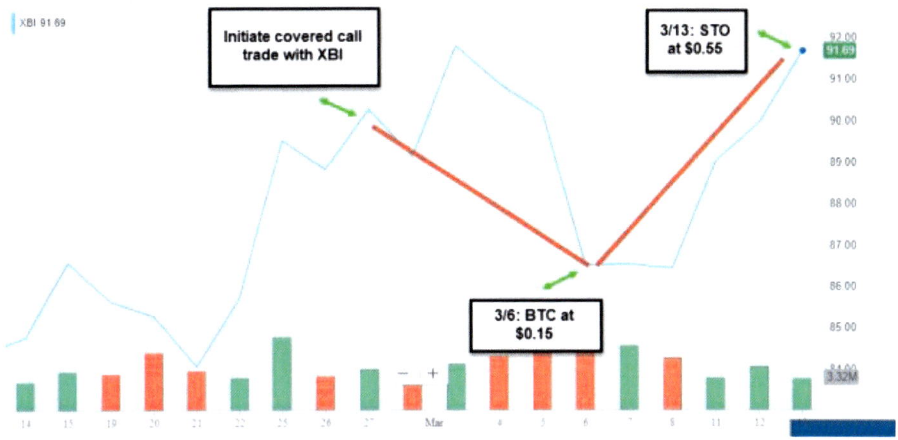

Figure 13: XBI: Hitting a Double V-Shaped Chart Pattern

Initial trade entries

Stock Symbol	Industry	Entry Trade Date	ER Date	Ex-Div Date	Entry Trade Expiry Date	Entry Stock Price [$/sh]	Entry Call Strike Price [$]	Entry Call Option Premium [$/sh]	Number Of Shares [#]
XBI	Biotech	02/26/19	NA	NA	03/21/19	$ 90.25	$ 92.00	$ 1.50	100

Figure 14: XBI: Entering Our Initial Trade

Initial trade returns with 10% guideline

OPENING TRADE								
Expected # Of Days In Trade [#]	Time-Value Per-Share [$/sh]	Intrinsic-Value Per-Share [$/sh]	Upside Value Per-Share [$/sh]	Breakeven Value Per-Share [$/sh]	Return On Option ROO [%]	Return On Option ROO Annual'zd [%]	Upside Potential [%]	Downside Protect. [%]
24	$ 1.50	$ -	$ 1.75	$ 88.75	1.66%	25.28%	1.94%	0.00%

Trade ROO Premium [$]	Trade Upside Premium [$]	Total Capital Invested [$]	20% Option Exit Guideline [$]	10% Option Exit Guideline [$]	7% Stock Exit Guideline [$]
$ 150.00	$ 175.00	$ 9,025.00	$ 0.30	$ 0.15	$ 83.93

Figure 15: XBI: Initial Trade Returns

The spreadsheet shows an initial time-value return of 1.66%, 25.28% annualized based on a 24-day trade with an additional upside potential profit of 1.94% if share price moves up to the $92.00 out-of-the-money call strike. The 10% guideline threshold is $0.15.

Trade adjustment entries

EXIT STRATEGY TRA									
Stock Symbol	Exit Strategy Selected	Adjust. Trade Date	Adjust. Expiry Date	BTC Entry Option Price [$/Sh]	STO Entry #2 Strike Price [$]	STO Entry #2 Option Premium [$/Sh]	Final Stock Sale Price If Sold [$/Sh]	Final Unsold Stock Price [$/Sh]
XBI	Hit Double/Keep Stock	03/06/19		$ 0.15	$ 92.00	$ 0.55		$ 91.69

Figure 16: XBI: Exit Strategy Adjustments

Hitting a Double generated a net credit of $40.00 per-contract ($55.00 - $15.00). The final unsold stock price at expiration was $91.69.

Final calculations

Final Net Option Profit/Loss [$/Sh]	Final Net Option Profit/Loss [$]	Final Net Option Return [%]	Realized Final Stock Profit/Loss per share [$/Sh]	Realized Final $ Total Stock Profit/Loss [$]	Realized Final Stock Profit/Loss [%]	Unrealized Final Stock Profit/Loss [$/Sh]	Unrealized Final Stock $ Total Stock Profit/Loss [$]	Unreal. Final Stock % Total Stock Profit/Loss [%]
$ 1.90	$ 190.00	2.11%	$ -	$ -	-	$ 1.44	$ 144.00	1.60%

FINAL RESULT	
Combined Final Trade Total Profit/Loss [$]	Combined Final Trade Total Profit/Loss [%]
$ 334.00	3.70%

Figure 17: XBI: Final Results After *Hitting a Double*

The final trade result after trade adjustments is 3.70%. This includes an unrealized share appreciation of $1.44 per-share or 1.60%. Shares are retained at the current market value of $91.69.

Discussion

The *hitting a double* exit strategy improved an initial time-value return of 1.70% to a final return of 3.70%. This includes an unrealized share appreciation of 1.60%. Shares are retained after expiration and a decision is made prior to market opening the next week regarding the sale or retention of XBI.

Chapter 6

Hitting a Double and Selling the Stock

What is hitting a double and selling the stock?

Hitting a double and then selling the underlying security involves buying back the short call using our 20%/10% guidelines and then re-selling that same option when share price recovers. The post-exit strategy chart will show a classic V-shaped pattern where share price first declines and then recovers. This creates 2 income streams in the same contract period with the same underlying security and investment. If the strike expires ITM and no action is taken to close the short call, the shares will be sold after contract expiration (usually on the Saturday after expiration Friday and our shares will no longer be in our broker accounts on the Monday after contract expiration).

When to consider hitting a double and selling the shares

We, generally, use this exit strategy in the first half of a monthly contract (there are exceptions and used later in a contract) when share price declines and there is adequate time for share price recovery. The decision to allow exercise and sell our shares at expiration is made at the end of a contract. If a strike is expiring OTM, the exit strategy designation is, then, *hitting a double* and retaining the stock. Shares can then be sold the Monday after expiration Friday.

Real-life example with SPDR S&P Biotech ETF (NYSE: XBI)

- 2/26/2019: 300 shares XBI purchased at $90.25
- 2/26/2019: Sell-to-open 1 contract of the March 21, 2019 $92.00 calls at $1.50
- 3/6/2019: Buy-to-close the $92.00 calls at $0.15 (10% guideline)
- 3/13/2019: Sell-to-open the $92.00 calls at $0.55
- 3/21/2019: XBI price is $92.69 at expiration
- 3/21/2019: $92.00 calls were allowed to be exercised and shares sold at $92.00

Initial trade entries

Stock Symbol	Industry	Entry Trade Date	ER Date	Ex-Div Date	Entry Trade Expiry Date	Entry Stock Price [$/sh]	Entry Call Strike Price [$]	Entry Call Option Premium [$/sh]	Number Of Shares [#]
XBI	Biotech	02/26/19	NA	NA	03/21/19	$ 90.25	$ 92.00	$ 1.50	100

Figure 18: XBI: Entering Our Initial Trade

Initial trade returns

OPENING TRADE								
Expected # Of Days In Trade [#]	Time-Value Per-Share [$/sh]	Intrinsic-Value Per-Share [$/sh]	Upside Value Per-Share [$/sh]	Breakeven Value Per-Share [$/sh]	Return On Option ROO [%]	Return On Option ROO Annual'zd [%]	Upside Potential [%]	Downside Protect. [%]
24	$ 1.50	$ -	$ 1.75	$ 88.75	1.66%	25.28%	1.94%	0.00%

Trade ROO Premium [$]	Trade Upside Premium [$]	Total Capital Invested [$]	20% Option Exit Guideline [$]	10% Option Exit Guideline [$]	7% Stock Exit Guideline [$]
$ 150.00	$ 175.00	$ 9,025.00	$ 0.30	$ 0.15	$ 83.93

Figure 19: XBI: Initial Trade Returns

The spreadsheet shows an initial time-value return of 1.66%, 25.28% annualized based on a 24-day trade with an additional upside potential profit of 1.94% if share price moves up to the $92.00 out-of-the-money call strike.

Trade adjustment entries

Stock Symbol	Exit Strategy Selected	Adjust. Trade Date	Adjust. Expiry Date	BTC Entry Option Price [$/Sh]	STO Entry #2 Strike Price [$]	STO Entry #2 Option Premium [$/Sh]	Final Stock Sale Price If Sold [$/Sh]	Final Unsold Stock Price [$/Sh]
XBI	Hit Double/Sell Stock	03/06/19		$ 0.15	$ 92.00	$ 0.55	$ 92.00	

Figure 20: XBI: Hitting a Double Trade Adjustments

Hitting a Double generated a new credit of $40.00 per-contract ($55.00 - $15.00). At expiration, with the $92.00 strike now in-the-money, exercise resulted in shares being sold at $92.00.

Final calculations

Final Net Option Profit/Loss [$/Sh]	Final Net Option Profit/Loss [$]	Final Net Option Return [%]	Realized Final Stock Profit/Loss per share [$/Sh]	Realized Final $ Total Stock Profit/Loss [$]	Realized Final Stock Profit/Loss [%]	Unrealized Final Stock Profit/Loss [$/Sh]	Unrealized Final Stock $ Total Stock Profit/Loss [$]	Unreal. Final Stock % Total Stock Profit/Loss [%]
$ 1.90	$ 190.00	2.11%	$ 1.75	$ 175.00	1.94%	$ -	$ -	

FINAL RESULT	
Combined Final Trade Total Profit/Loss [$]	Combined Final Trade Total Profit/Loss [%]
$ 365.00	4.04%

Figure 21: XBI: Final Results After Hitting a Double and Shares are Sold

The final trade resulted in a realized option return of 2.11% and a realized stock return of 1.94%, for a total net realized 24-day profit of 4.04%.

Discussion

The *hitting a double* exit strategy improved an initial time-value return of 1.70% to a final return of 4.04%. This includes a realized share appreciation of 1.94%.

Chapter 7

Mid-Contract Unwind Exit Strategy

What is the mid-contract unwind exit strategy?

After entering our covered call trades and share price rises substantially, there are often opportunities to generate a 2nd income stream by closing both legs of the original trade and entering a new one with a different underlying security. In the BCI methodology, this is known as the *Mid-Contract Unwind* (MCU) exit strategy. We will highlight an example of this strategy using Nucor Corp. (NYSE: NUE).

When to consider using the mid-contract unwind exit strategy

This position management technique is generally applied in the first half of a monthly contract although it can be used in the second half, particularly in volatile market conditions. These opportunities arise when share value appreciates significantly after entering a covered call trade causing the *time-value* component of the premium to approach zero as shown in Figure 22. *If we can generate at least 1% more than the time-value cost-to-close the initial call by contract expiration, then the MCU exit strategy should be considered.*

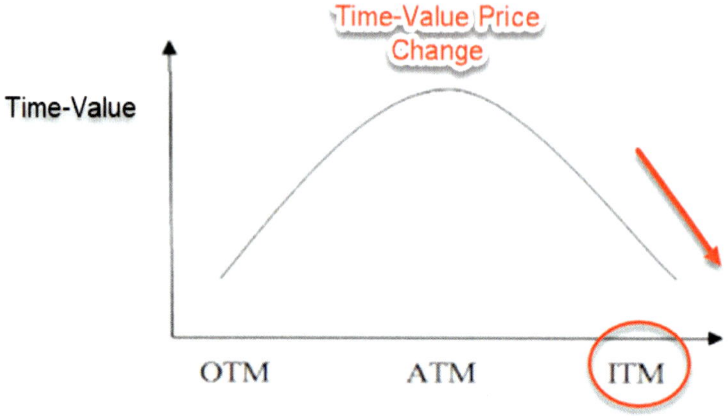

Figure 22: Time-Value Approaches Zero as Call Strike Moves Deeper ITM

Real-life example with NUE

- 7/25/2021: Buy 100 x NUE at $96.87
- 7/25/2021: STO the 8/20/2021 ITM $95.00 call at $4.90
- 8/6/2021: BTC the 8/20/2021 $95.00 call at $9.70
- 8/6/2021: Sell 100 x NUE at $104.28

Initial trade entries

Stock Symbol	Industry	Entry Trade Date	ER Date	Ex-Div Date	Entry Trade Expiry Date	Entry Stock Price [$/sh]	Entry Call Strike Price [$]	Entry Call Option Premium [$/sh]	Number Of Shares [#]
NUE	Materials	07/25/21	08/21/21	08/28/21	08/20/21	$ 96.87	$ 95.00	$ 4.90	100

Figure 23: NUE: Initial Trade Entries

Initial trade returns

OPENING TRADE						
Expected # Of Days In Trade [#]	Time-Value Per-Share [$/sh]	Intrinsic-Value Per-Share [$/sh]	Upside Value Per-Share [$/sh]	Breakeven Value Per-Share [$/sh]	Return On Option ROO [%]	Return On Option ROO Annual'zd [%]
27	$ 3.03	$ 1.87	$ -	$ 91.97	3.19%	43.12%

Upside Potential [%]	Downside Protect. [%]	Trade ROO Premium [$]	Trade Upside Premium [$]	Total Capital Invested [$]
0.00%	1.93%	$ 303.00	$ -	$ 9,500.00

Figure 24: NUE: Initial Trade Returns

The spreadsheet shows an initial time-value return of 3.19%, 43.12% annualized based on a 27-day trade with 1.93% downside protection of that initial time-value return (intrinsic-value protects time-value). Since the option sold was in-the-money, no additional profit (upside potential) can be gleaned from share appreciation.

How to manage our trade adjustments

We enter the BTC price to close the short call and the price of the shares sold (current market value) after eliminating the option contract obligation.

Trade adjustment entries

EXIT STRATEGY TRA								
Stock Symbol	Exit Strategy Selected	Adjust. Trade Date	Adjust. Expiry Date	BTC Entry Option Price [$/Sh]	STO Entry #2 Strike Price [$]	STO Entry #2 Option Premium [$/Sh]	Final Stock Sale Price If Sold [$/Sh]	Final Unsold Stock Price [$/Sh]
NUE	Mid-Contract Unwind (MCU)	08/06/21		$ 9.70			$ 104.28	

Figure 25: NUE: MCU Exit Strategy Adjustments

Final calculations

Final Net Option Profit/Loss [$/Sh]	Final Net Option Profit/Loss [$]	Final Net Option Return [%]	Realized Final Stock Profit/Loss per share [$/Sh]	Realized Final $ Total Stock Profit/Loss [$]	Realized Final Stock Profit/Loss [%]	Unrealized Final Stock Profit/Loss [$/Sh]	Unrealized Final Stock $ Total Stock Profit/Loss [$]	Unreal. Final Stock % Total Stock Profit/Loss [%]
$ (4.80)	$ (480.00)	-4.96%	$ 7.41	$ 741.00	7.65%	$ -	$ -	

FINAL RESULT	
Combined Final Trade Total Profit/Loss [$]	Combined Final Trade Total Profit/Loss [%]
$ 261.00	2.69%

Figure 26: NUE: Final Returns After Executing the MCU Strategy

The final trade result after trade adjustments is 2.69% factoring in share appreciation (7.65%) and option debit (-4.96%). The cash created by the sale of NUE is now available to generate a second income stream in the same contract month with the same cash investment. The additional cash needed to close the original short call is mitigated by the share appreciation after removal of the cap created by the short call.

This exit strategy implies a second option trade in the same expiration period. See the Chapter 14, on the topic of using multiple exit strategies, to learn how to enter these additional trades in the same contract cycle into our trading log spreadsheets.

Discussion

The MCU exit strategy resulted in a time-value cost-to-close of 0.44% (3.19% – 2.75%). This factors in the intrinsic-value component of the $9.70 cost-to-close (CTC):

Time-value CTC: [($9.70 – ($104.28 - $95.00)]/$95.00 = 0.44%

We use this exit strategy when we can generate at least 1% more than this time-value cost-to-close or 1.44% or higher by the end of the same contract expiration.

Chapter 8

Rolling-Down/Keeping Stock

What is rolling-down and keeping the stock?

Rolling-down is one of our frequently used covered call writing exit strategies. When we roll-down, we buy back the original short call and sell another at a lower strike with the same contract expiration. This will generate a net option credit but also place a ceiling on the potential value of the underlying security at contract expiration. We typically use this strategy to mitigate the debit in a losing trade.

At the end of the contract the shares are retained in our portfolios by either closing an ITM strike at expiration or allowing the option to expire worthless, if OTM at expiration. During the January 2022 contracts, there was a 5% market decline due to COVD-19, inflation and interest rate concerns. This example will highlight a rolling-down strategy implemented with Healthcare Select Sector SPDR (NYSE: XLV), in one of my portfolios, where a 4.68% share loss was mitigated down to a 2.8% loss. In this example, we will run the calculations assuming shares were retained at the end of the contract.

When to consider rolling-down and keeping the stock

This exit strategy is implemented when share value declines causing our 20%/10% BTC limit order thresholds to be reached and executed and a decision is made to manage, rather than sell, the underlying shares. These shares will be retained if the lower strike is OTM at expiration or if we decide to roll (out) an ITM strike as expiration approaches. Rolling-out management will be discussed later in this book.

Real-life example with XLV

- 12/21/2021: Buy 100 x XLV at $135.83
- 12/21/2021: STO 1 x $137.50 1/21/2022 call at $2.20
- 1/7/2022: BTC 1 x 1/21/2022 $137.50 call at $0.44 (20% guideline)
- 1/11/2022: STO 1 x 1/21/2022 $136.50 calls (rolling-down) at $0.80
- 1/21/2022: XLV shares worth $129.47 (a stock loss of 4.68%) and retained for an unrealized loss as the $136.50 strike expires worthless and OTM.

Initial trade entries

Stock Symbol	Industry	Entry Trade Date	ER Date	Ex-Div Date	Entry Trade Expiry Date	Entry Stock Price [$/sh]	Entry Call Strike Price [$]	Entry Call Option Premium [$/sh]	Number Of Shares [#]
XLV	Health	12/21/21	NA	12/20/21	01/21/22	$ 135.83	$ 137.50	$ 2.20	100

Figure 27: XLV: Initial Trade Entries

Initial trade returns and the 20% guideline

OPENING TRADE								
Expected # Of Days In Trade [#]	Time-Value Per-Share [$/sh]	Intrinsic-Value Per-Share [$/sh]	Upside Value Per-Share [$/sh]	Breakeven Value Per-Share [$/sh]	Return On Option ROO [%]	Return On Option ROO Annual'zd [%]	Upside Potential [%]	Downside Protect. [%]
32	$ 2.20	$ -	$ 1.67	$ 133.63	1.62%	18.47%	1.23%	0.00%

Trade ROO Premium [$]	Trade Upside Premium [$]	Total Capital Invested [$]	20% Option Exit Guideline [$]	10% Option Exit Guideline [$]	7% Stock Exit Guideline [$]
$ 220.00	$ 167.00	$ 13,583.00	$ 0.44	$ 0.22	$ 126.32

Figure 28: XLV: Initial Trade Returns

The spreadsheet shows an initial time-value return of 1.62%, 18.47% annualized based on a 32-day trade. There is also upside potential of 1.23%. The 20% BTC limit order threshold is $0.44

How to manage rolling-down and keeping the stock trades

Enter the date of the trade adjustment, the BTC and STO premiums and the new lower strike price. We also enter the value of the unsold stock at expiration (the lower of current market value or the strike, if ITM).

Trade adjustment entries

Stock Symbol	Exit Strategy Selected	Adjust. Trade Date	Adjust. Expiry Date	BTC Entry Option Price [$/Sh]	STO Entry #2 Strike Price [$]	STO Entry #2 Option Premium [$/Sh]	Final Stock Sale Price If Sold [$/Sh]	Final Unsold Stock Price [$/Sh]
XLV	Roll-Down/Keep Stock	01/07/22		$ 0.44	$ 136.50	$ 0.80		$ 129.47

Figure 29: XLV: Rolling-Down Adjustments

Final calculations

Final Stock Sale Price If Sold [$/Sh]	Final Unsold Stock Price [$/Sh]	Final Net Option Profit/Loss [$/Sh]	Final Net Option Profit/Loss [$]	Final Net Option Return [%]	Realized Final Stock Profit/Loss per share [$/Sh]	Realized Final $ Total Stock Profit/Loss [$]	Realized Final Stock Profit/Loss [%]	Unrealized Final Stock Profit/Loss [$/Sh]	Unrealized Final Stock $ Total Stock Profit/Loss [$]	Unreal. Final Stock % Total Stock Profit/Loss [%]
	$ 129.47	$ 2.56	$ 256.00	1.88%	$ -	$ -	-	$ (6.36)	$ (636.00)	-4.68%

FINAL RESULT	
Combined Final Trade Total Profit/Loss [$]	Combined Final Trade Total Profit/Loss [%]
$ (380.00)	-2.80%

Figure 30: XLV: Final Results After Rolling-Down

The spreadsheet shows a net option credit of 1.88% and a net stock unrealized (shares are yet sold) loss of 4.68% for a total position unrealized loss of 2.80%.

Discussion

Writing covered calls and then mitigating losses by rolling-down decreased a 4.68% loss in share value down to an unrealized loss of 2.80% due to an option net credit of $256.00 or 1.88%. During the weekend after expiration Friday, a decision is made regarding the continued use or sale of XLV for the next contract cycle.

Chapter 9

Rolling-Down/Selling Stock

What is rolling-down and selling the stock?

Rolling-down is one of our frequently used covered call writing exit strategies. When we roll-down, we buy back the original short call and sell another at a lower strike with the same contract expiration. This will generate a net option credit but also put a ceiling on the potential value of the underlying security at contract expiration. Prior to the end of the contract the shares are sold after closing the short call or allowing exercise of an ITM strike. Shares can also be sold immediately after contract expiration.

During the January 2022 contracts, there was a 5% market decline due to COVD-19, inflation and interest rate concerns. This example will highlight a rolling-down strategy implemented with Healthcare Select Sector SPDR (NYSE: XLV) where a 4.68% share loss was mitigated down to a 2.8% loss. In this case, we will run the calculations assuming shares were sold just prior to contract expiration and the time-value cost-to-close the short call was near $0.00.

When to consider rolling-down and selling the stock

This exit strategy is implemented when share value declines causing our 20%/10% BTC limit orders to be executed and a decision is made to manage, rather than sell, the shares. Shares will ultimately be sold if we decide that our portfolio will benefit from a better-performing underlying security in the following contract cycle.

Real-life example with XLV

- 12/20/2021: Buy 100 x XLV at $135.83
- 12/20/2021: STO 1 x $137.50 1/21/2022 call at $2.20
- 1/7/2022: BTC 1 x 1/21/2022 $137.50 calls at $0.44 (20% guideline)
- 1/11/2022: STO 1 1/21/2022 $136.50 calls (rolling-down) at $0.80
- 1/21/2022: XLV shares worth $129.47 (a loss of 4.68%) and sold for a realized loss as the $136.50 strike expires OTM. The cost-to-close the short call was $0.01, negligible to our final calculations.

Initial trade entries

Stock Symbol	Industry	Entry Trade Date	ER Date	Ex-Div Date	Entry Trade Expiry Date	Entry Stock Price [$/sh]	Entry Call Strike Price [$]	Entry Call Option Premium [$/sh]	Number Of Shares [#]
XLV	Health	12/20/21	NA	12/20/21	01/21/22	$ 135.83	$ 137.50	$ 2.20	100

Figure 31: XLV: Entering Our Initial Trade

Initial trade returns and the 20% BTC limit order

OPENING TRADE								
Expected # Of Days In Trade [#]	Time-Value Per-Share [$/sh]	Intrinsic-Value Per-Share [$/sh]	Upside Value Per-Share [$/sh]	Breakeven Value Per-Share [$/sh]	Return On Option ROO [%]	Return On Option ROO Annual'zd [%]	Upside Potential [%]	Downside Protect. [%]
32	$ 2.20	$ -	$ 1.67	$ 133.63	1.62%	18.47%	1.23%	0.00%

Trade ROO Premium [$]	Trade Upside Premium [$]	Total Capital Invested [$]	20% Option Exit Guideline [$]	10% Option Exit Guideline [$]	7% Stock Exit Guideline [$]
$ 220.00	$ 167.00	$ 13,583.00	$ 0.44	$ 0.22	$ 126.32

Figure 32: XLV: Initial Trade Returns and the 20% Guideline

The spreadsheet shows an initial time-value return of 1.62%, 18.47% annualized based on a 32-day trade. There is also upside potential of 1.23%. The 20% BTC limit order threshold is set at $0.44.

How to manage our rolling-down and selling the stock trades

The trade adjustment date, BTC and STO option premiums, new lower strike price and final sale price of the stock are entered into the spreadsheet.

Trade adjustment entries

Stock Symbol	Exit Strategy Selected	Adjust. Trade Date	Adjust. Expiry Date	BTC Entry Option Price [$/Sh]	STO Entry #2 Strike Price [$]	STO Entry #2 Option Premium [$/Sh]	Final Stock Sale Price If Sold [$/Sh]	Final Unsold Stock Price [$/Sh]
XLV	Roll-Down/Sell Stock	01/07/22		$ 0.44	$ 136.50	$ 0.80	$ 129.47	

Figure 33: XLV: Rolling-Down Adjustment Entries

Final calculations

Final Net Option Profit/Loss [$/Sh]	Final Net Option Profit/Loss [$]	Final Net Option Return [%]	Realized Final Stock Profit/Loss per share [$/Sh]	Realized Final $ Total Stock Profit/Loss [$]	Realized Final Stock Profit/Loss [%]	Unrealized Final Stock Profit/Loss [$/Sh]	Unrealized Final Stock $ Total Stock Profit/Loss [$]	Unreal. Final Stock % Total Stock Profit/Loss [%]
$ 2.56	$ 256.00	1.88%	$ (6.36)	$ (636.00)	-4.68%	$ -	$ -	

FINAL RESULT	
Combined Final Trade Total Profit/Loss [$]	Combined Final Trade Total Profit/Loss [%]
$ (380.00)	-2.80%

Figure 34: XLV: Rolling-Down Final Calculations

The spreadsheet shows a net option credit of 1.88% and a net stock realized (shares are sold) loss of 4.68% for a total position realized loss of 2.80%.

To get a 100% accurate calculation by factoring in the miniscule time-value cost-to-close of the lower strike, simply deduct it from the second option premium. In this example, change the STO Entry #2 from $0.80 to $0.79.

Discussion

Writing covered calls and then mitigating losses by rolling-down decreased a 4.68% loss in share value down to a realized loss of 2.80% due to an option net credit of $256.00 or 1.88%. Position management is the 3rd of the 3 required skills (along with stock and option selection) that must be mastered before risking even one penny of our hard-earned money.

Chapter 10

Rolling-In

What is rolling-in?

Closing out options at a current-term expiration and opening at the same strike at an earlier date. This is a *new exit strategy term, developed by BCI,* as a result of experiencing situations when shortening a contract expiration date to a nearer-term expiration will mitigate risk with other potential benefits.

When to consider rolling-in

Avoid risky corporate or market events

- Earnings reports
- Fed announcement
- FDA product announcement
- Corporate news conference
- Political events

Personal business commitments: unavailable to monitor trades

- Family vacation
- Business trip
- Hospital stays/medical reasons

Must liquidate position by a specific date

- Cash needed for other obligations

Real-life example with Etsy, Inc. (NASDAQ: ETSY)

- 2/15/2021: Buy 100 x ETSY at $233.86
- 2/15/2021: STO 1 x 3/19/2021 $240.00 call at $16.90
- 2/22/2021: BTC 1 x 3/19/2021 $240.00 call at $17.60
- 2/22/2021: STO 1 x 3/12/2021 $240.00 call at $15.50
- 3/12/2021: ETSY trading at $242.11 and exercise is allowed as shares are sold at the $240.00 strike

Initial trade entries

Stock Symbol	Industry	Entry Trade Date	ER Date	Ex-Div Date	Entry Trade Expiry Date	Entry Stock Price [$/sh]	Entry Call Strike Price [$]	Entry Call Option Premium [$/sh]	Number Of Shares [#]
ETSY	Int. Retail	02/15/21	05/26/21	NA	03/19/21	$ 233.86	$ 240.00	$ 16.90	100

Figure 35: ETSY: Initial Trade Entries

Initial trade returns

OPENING TRADE						
Expected # Of Days In Trade [#]	Time-Value Per-Share [$/sh]	Intrinsic-Value Per-Share [$/sh]	Upside Value Per-Share [$/sh]	Breakeven Value Per-Share [$/sh]	Return On Option ROO [%]	Return On Option ROO Annual'zd [%]
33	$ 16.90	$ -	$ 6.14	$ 216.96	7.23%	79.93%

Upside Potential [%]	Downside Protect. [%]	Trade ROO Premium [$]	Trade Upside Premium [$]	Total Capital Invested [$]
2.63%	0.00%	$ 1,690.00	$ 614.00	$ 23,386.00

Figure 36: ETSY: Initial Trade

The spreadsheet shows an initial return on the option (ROO) of 7.23% and a 79.93% annualized based on a 33-day trade. Plus, there is an additional upside potential of 2.63%, should share price rise to the $240.00 OTM strike, by expiration. The total potential maximum 33-day return is 9.86%.

How to manage rolling-in trades

Enter the trade adjustment date, the new, shorter-term expiration date, The BTC and STO option premiums, the same strike price and the final sold or unsold price of the stock.

Trade adjustment entries

Stock Symbol	Exit Strategy Selected	Adjust. Trade Date	Adjust. Expiry Date	BTC Entry Option Price [$/Sh]	STO Entry #2 Strike Price [$]	STO Entry #2 Option Premium [$/Sh]	Final Stock Sale Price If Sold [$/Sh]	Final Unsold Stock Price [$/Sh]
ETSY	Roll-In	02/22/21	03/12/21	$ 17.60	$ 240.00	$ 15.50	$ 240.00	$ -

Figure 37: ETSY: Rolling-In Adjustments

The 3/19/2021 expiration is rolled-in to the 3/12/2021 expiration resulting in a net option debit of $$2.10 ($17.60 - $15.50).

Final calculations

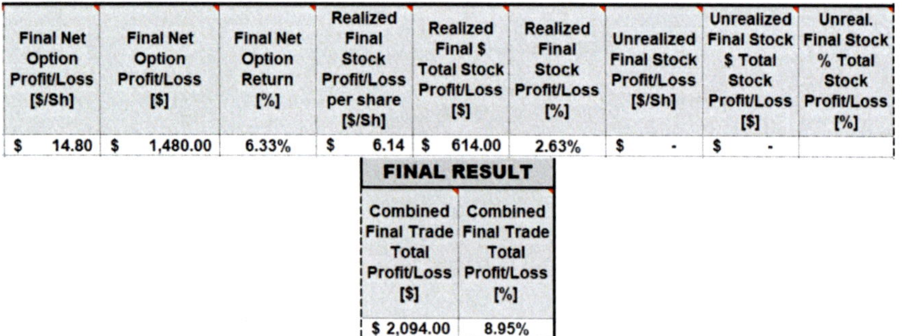

Final Net Option Profit/Loss [$/Sh]	Final Net Option Profit/Loss [$]	Final Net Option Return [%]	Realized Final Stock Profit/Loss per share [$/Sh]	Realized Final $ Total Stock Profit/Loss [$]	Realized Final Stock Profit/Loss [%]	Unrealized Final Stock Profit/Loss [$/Sh]	Unrealized Final Stock $ Total Stock Profit/Loss [$]	Unreal. Final Stock % Total Stock Profit/Loss [%]
$ 14.80	$ 1,480.00	6.33%	$ 6.14	$ 614.00	2.63%	$ -	$ -	

FINAL RESULT	
Combined Final Trade Total Profit/Loss [$]	Combined Final Trade Total Profit/Loss [%]
$ 2,094.00	8.95%

Figure 38: ETSY: Final Results After rolling-In

The spreadsheet shows a final combined stock and option return of 8.95%, slightly lower than the initial maximum return of 9.86%. Keep in mind that the cash involved in the trade will have an additional week to be re-invested, using a different underlying security, to mitigate this minor decrease in the maximum return. However, the exit strategy avoided a potential risky event (strategy assumption) in the final week of the March contracts.

Discussion

Rolling-in is an additional position management technique that can be utilized to avoid risky events as well as allow for better management and needs. The cost to roll-in will typically be low or may even result in a higher annualized return but will always mitigate the overall risk inherent in our portfolio positions. However, to be useful, the underlying security will, generally, need to have weekly options (some exceptions if initial trade expirations are several months out).

Chapter 11

Rolling-Out

What is rolling-out?

When rolling our covered call writing trades out, we close the near-month in-the-money (ITM) call and sell a same strike option in the next contract cycle. When rolling-out ITM strikes, we are always *rolling-out to ITM strikes at a later expiration date at the time of the roll* (with some extremely rare exceptions). If using Monthly options, this becomes a 2-month trade as initially structured. The dilemma becomes how to enter these trades into our trading log when measuring monthly results (can be other time frames, as well). We will use a real-life example with United Therapeutics Corp., Inc. (Nasdaq: UTHR) to explain this strategy.

When to consider rolling-out

We consider this exit strategy opportunity when the original covered call strike is expiring ITM and the underlying security still meets our system requirements, including no upcoming earnings report in the next contract cycle. The rolling calculations must also align with our stated initial time-value return goal range.

Real-life example with UTHR

- 2/22/21: Buy 100 x UTHR at $155.90
- 2/22/21: STO 1 x 3/21/2021 $150.00 (ITM) call at $9.25

- 3/21/2021: UTHR trading at 163.22
- 3/21/2021: BTC the 3/21/2021 $150.00 call at $15.50
- 3/21/2021: STO the 4/18/2021 $150.00 (rolling-out to an ITM strike) at $18.75

Initial trade entries

Stock Symbol	Industry	Entry Trade Date	ER Date	Ex-Div Date	Entry Trade Expiry Date	Entry Stock Price [$/sh]	Entry Call Strike Price [$]	Entry Call Option Premium [$/sh]	Number Of Shares [#]
UTHR	Healthcare	02/22/21	04/20/21	NA	03/21/21	$ 155.90	$ 150.00	$ 9.25	100

Figure 39: UTHR: Entering Our Initial Trade

Initial trade returns

OPENING TRADE						
Expected # Of Days In Trade [#]	Time-Value Per-Share [$/sh]	Intrinsic-Value Per-Share [$/sh]	Upside Value Per-Share [$/sh]	Breakeven Value Per-Share [$/sh]	Return On Option ROO [%]	Return On Option ROO Annual'zd [%]
28	$ 3.35	$ 5.90	$ -	$ 146.65	2.23%	29.11%

Upside Potential [%]	Downside Protect. [%]	Trade ROO Premium [$]	Trade Upside Premium [$]	Total Capital Invested [$]
0.00%	3.78%	$ 335.00	$ -	$ 15,000.00

Figure 40: UTHR: Initial Trade Returns

The spreadsheet shows an initial time-value return of 2.23%, 29.11% annualized based on a 28-day trade, with 3.78% downside protection of that initial profit. The breakeven price point is $146.65 (yellow cell).

How to manage these situations

Since the strike is ITM as expiration approaches, the initial trade return is maximized. We enter the final stock's unrealized value as the ITM strike because that is what the shares are, in fact, worth due to our contract obligation to sell at that price. We, then, *enter the rolling aspect of the trade into the next contract cycle, using the initial strike as share value and the combined net buy-to-close and sell-to-open rolling premiums as the option premium for the next contract cycle*. This will result in a net option credit.

Trade adjustment entries

Stock Symbol	Exit Strategy Selected	Adjust. Trade Date	Adjust. Expiry Date	BTC Entry Option Price [$/Sh]	STO Entry #2 Strike Price [$]	STO Entry #2 Option Premium [$/Sh]	Final Stock Sale Price If Sold [$/Sh]	Final Unsold Stock Price [$/Sh]
UTHR	Roll Out	03/21/21						$ 150.00

Figure 41: UTHR: Adjustments Prior to Rolling-Out

Shares are valued at $150.00, the original strike price prior to rolling-out.

Final calculations

Final Net Option Profit/Loss [$/Sh]	Final Net Option Profit/Loss [$]	Final Net Option Return [%]	Realized Final Stock Profit/Loss per share [$/Sh]	Realized Final $ Total Stock Profit/Loss [$]	Realized Final Stock Profit/Loss [%]	Unrealized Final Stock Profit/Loss [$/Sh]	Unrealized Final Stock $ Total Stock Profit/Loss [$]	Unreal. Final Stock % Total Stock Profit/Loss [%]
$ 9.25	$ 925.00	5.93%	$ -	$ -	-	$ (5.90)	$ (590.00)	-3.78%

FINAL RESULT	
Combined Final Trade Total Profit/Loss [$]	Combined Final Trade Total Profit/Loss [%]
$ 335.00	2.15%

Figure 42: UTHR: Final Results Prior to Rolling-Out

The final pre-roll return is 2.15%. This includes an option credit of $925.00 (5.93%) and an unrealized stock debit of $590.00 (-3.78%) on an original cost-basis of $155.90. *Note that when we calculate initial calculations, we deduct intrinsic-value for ITM strikes to calculate our cost-basis. When we calculate final returns, we use the original cost of the shares for ITM strikes, the same as we use for ATM and OTM strikes. The reason is that we are using the total option premium for final calculations, whereas we used only the time-value component for initial calculations. This explains the slight difference between the initial returns (2.23%) and the final pre-roll return (2.15%).* Here is an exaggerated hypothetical example to highlight how this works.

A hypothetical example of ITM initial and final calculations

- BCI trading at $100.00
- STO $90.00 call at $12.00 ($10.00 intrinsic-value + $2.00 time-value)

- There will be a $10.00 loss in share value due to the contract obligation to sell at $90.00
- Initial calculation return: Time-value of premium ($2.00)/ (Share price – intrinsic-value of premium) … $2.00/$90.00 = 2.2%
- Final calculation (if no changes): Entire premium/ Share price … $12.00/$100.00 = 12%
- Our shares are now worth $90.00, not $100.00 and this loss will be debited in the rolled-out trade in the next contract cycle

Now, back to the UTHR example.

Entering our rolling-out trades into the next contract cycle

Stock Symbol	Industry	Entry Trade Date	ER Date	Ex-Div Date	Entry Trade Expiry Date	Entry Stock Price [$/sh]	Entry Call Strike Price [$]	Entry Call Option Premium [$/sh]	Number Of Shares [#]
UTHR	Healthcare	03/21/21	04/20/21	NA	04/18/21	$ 150.00	$ 150.00	$ 3.25	100

Figure 43: UTHR: Entering the Roll-Out Trade in the Next Contract Cycle

The stock value is the price of the stock based on our previous contract obligation to sell at $150.00. The option credit is the cost-to-close the previous $150.00 strike and the premium received by selling the ITM $150.00 strike (based on current market value of $163.22). This trade resulted in a net credit of $3.25 per-share ($18.75 - $15.50).

Initial next contract calculations after rolling-out into the next contract cycle

OPENING TRADE						
Expected # Of Days In Trade [#]	Time-Value Per-Share [$/sh]	Intrinsic-Value Per-Share [$/sh]	Upside Value Per-Share [$/sh]	Breakeven Value Per-Share [$/sh]	Return On Option ROO [%]	Return On Option ROO Annual'zd [%]
29	$ 3.25	$ -	$ -	$ 146.75	2.17%	27.27%

Upside Potential [%]	Downside Protect. [%]	Trade ROO Premium [$]	Trade Upside Premium [$]	Total Capital Invested [$]
0.00%	0.00%	$ 325.00	$ -	$ 15,000.00

Figure 44: UTHR: Next Month Initial Calculations

The spreadsheet shows an option credit of 2.17%, 27.27% annualized based on a 29-day trade with the strike price ($150.00) now deep in-the-money (stock price at $163.22 at the time of the roll). The maximum return for the next contract month is 2.17%. *Although the spreadsheet will show no downside protection because the value of the shares at the time of the roll was the same as the rolled-out strike price, we actually do have protection from the current market value of $163.22 down to the $150.00 strike.* The reason the spreadsheet shows no downside protection is because we entered the practical value of our shares at the end of the previous contract ($150.00 due to our previous contract obligation) rather than actual current market value which is $163.22.

Discussion

When rolling our covered call trades, we close the current month trade by entering the (now) ITM strike as the final share value thereby maximizing the trade as initially structured. We then enter the next month, post adjustment, trade using the previous strike as our cost-basis and the net option credit with the new expiration date.

**** See Appendix IV for detailed information on entering & calculating rolling-out trades.*

Chapter 12

Rolling-Out-And-Up to an ITM Strike

What is rolling-out-and-up?

When rolling our covered call writing trades out-and-up, we close the near-month in-the-money (ITM) call and sell a higher strike option in the next contract cycle. This rolled-up strike can be ITM, ATM or OTM compared to current value of the underlying security. If using Monthly options, this becomes a 2-month trade as initially structured. The dilemma becomes how to enter these trades into our trading log when measuring monthly results (can be other time frames, as well). We will use a real-life example with United Therapeutics Corp., Inc. (Nasdaq: UTHR) to demonstrate this position management technique.

When to consider rolling out-and-up

We use this technique when the strike is ITM as expiration is approaching and the underlying security still meets of system screening requirements. This includes no upcoming earnings report in the next contract cycle. We also run preliminary calculations to assure the initial time-value returns align with our stated goals. Rolling-out-and-up is considered more bullish than simply rolling-out.

Real-life example with UTHR

- 2/22/21: Buy 100 x UTHR at $155.90
- 2/22/21: STO 1 x 3/19/21 $150.00 (ITM) call at $9.25
- 3/19/21: UTHR trading at 163.22
- 3/19/21: BTC the $150.00 call at $15.50
- 3/19/21: STO the 4/18/21 $160.00 (rolling out-and-up to an ITM strike) at $9.50

Initial trade entries

Stock Symbol	Industry	Entry Trade Date	ER Date	Ex-Div Date	Entry Trade Expiry Date	Entry Stock Price [$/sh]	Entry Call Strike Price [$]	Entry Call Option Premium [$/sh]	Number Of Shares [#]
UTHR	Healthcare	02/22/21	04/20/21	NA	03/19/21	$ 155.90	$ 150.00	$ 9.25	100

Figure 45: UTHR: Initial Trade Entries

Initial trade returns

OPENING TRADE						
Expected # Of Days In Trade [#]	Time-Value Per-Share [$/sh]	Intrinsic-Value Per-Share [$/sh]	Upside Value Per-Share [$/sh]	Breakeven Value Per-Share [$/sh]	Return On Option ROO [%]	Return On Option ROO Annual'zd [%]
26	$ 3.35	$ 5.90	$ -	$ 146.65	2.23%	31.35%

Upside Potential [%]	Downside Protect. [%]	Trade ROO Premium [$]	Trade Upside Premium [$]	Total Capital Invested [$]
0.00%	3.78%	$ 335.00	$ -	$ 15,000.00

Figure 46: UTHR: Initial Trade Returns

The initial time-value return is 2.23%, 31.35% based on a 26-day trade. There is 3.78% downside protection of the initial time-value profit. Since an ITM strike was sold, this also represents the maximum time-value return outside of exit strategy adjustments.

How to manage rolling-out trades

Since the strike is ITM as expiration approaches, the initial trade return is maximized. We enter the final stock value as the ITM strike because that is what the shares are, in fact, worth due to our contract obligation to sell at that price. We, then, *enter the rolling aspect of the trade into the next contract cycle,* using the initial strike as share value and the buy-to-close and sell-to-open rolling premiums as the net option premium for the next contract cycle. Frequently, this will be a net debit. If there is an option debit due to the intrinsic-value component of the cost-to-close premium, that loss is mitigated by unrealized share appreciation when the first ITM strike is closed (shares will be worth current market value, more than the $150.00 initial strike price).

Trade adjustment entries

Stock Symbol	Exit Strategy Selected	Adjust. Trade Date	Adjust. Expiry Date	BTC Entry Option Price [$/Sh]	STO Entry #2 Strike Price [$]	STO Entry #2 Option Premium [$/Sh]	Final Stock Sale Price If Sold [$/Sh]	Final Unsold Stock Price [$/Sh]
UTHR	Roll-Out-and-Up	03/21/21						$ 150.00

Figure 47: UTHR: Rolling-Out-And-Up Adjustments

Since the option is being rolled-out to the next contract cycle, the trade is considered closed and we enter the final stock value prior to rolling. This is represented by the ITM strike which is the maximum this underlying can be worth due to the contract obligation to sell at that price.

Final calculations (prior to rolling)

Final Net Option Profit/Loss [$/Sh]	Final Net Option Profit/Loss [$]	Final Net Option Return [%]	Realized Final Stock Profit/Loss per share [$/Sh]	Realized Final $ Total Stock Profit/Loss [$]	Realized Final Stock Profit/Loss [%]	Unrealized Final Stock Profit/Loss [$/Sh]	Unrealized Final Stock $ Total Stock Profit/Loss [$]	Unreal. Final Stock % Total Stock Profit/Loss [%]
$ 9.25	$ 925.00	5.93%	$ -	$ -	-	$ (5.90)	$ (590.00)	-3.78%

FINAL RESULT	
Combined Final Trade Total Profit/Loss [$]	Combined Final Trade Total Profit/Loss [%]
$ 335.00	2.15%

Figure 48: UTHR: Final Results Prior to Rolling-Out-And-Up

The final pre-roll return is 2.15%. This includes an option credit of $925.00 (5.93%) and an unrealized stock debit of $590.00 (-3.78%) on an original cost-basis of $155.90. Note that when we calculate initial time-value calculations, we deduct intrinsic-value of the total option premium for ITM strikes as our cost-basis. This is because we do not use the intrinsic-value as part of our time-value returns, instead we use it to" buy down" our cost-basis.

When we calculate final returns, we use the original cost of the shares for ITM strikes, the same as we use for ATM and OTM strikes. The reason is that when we calculate initial returns, we use only the time-value component of ITM premiums but when calculating final results, we use the entire option premiums. This explains the slight difference between the initial returns (2.23%) and the final pre-roll return (2.15%).

Entering the rolling-out-and-up trade into the next contract cycle

Stock Symbol	Industry	Entry Trade Date	ER Date	Ex-Div Date	Entry Trade Expiry Date	Entry Stock Price [$/sh]	Entry Call Strike Price [$]	Entry Call Option Premium [$/sh]	Number Of Shares [#]
UTHR	Healthcare	03/19/21	05/26/21	NA	04/18/21	$ 150.00	$ 160.00	$ (6.00)	100

Figure 49: UTHR: Rolled-Out-And-Up-Trade Entries

The stock value is the price of the stock based on our previous contract obligation to sell at $150.00 (at the time of the roll, shares can be worth no more than the ITM strike). The option credit/debit (debit, in this case) is the cost-to-close the previous $150.00 strike and the premium received by selling the ITM $160.00 strike (based on current market value of $163.22). This resulted in an option debit of (-) $6.00.

Initial next contract calculations after rolling-out-and-up into the next contract cycle

OPENING TRADE						
Expected # Of Days In Trade [#]	Time-Value Per-Share [$/sh]	Intrinsic-Value Per-Share [$/sh]	Upside Value Per-Share [$/sh]	Breakeven Value Per-Share [$/sh]	Return On Option ROO [%]	Return On Option ROO Annual'zd [%]
31	$ (6.00)	$ -	$ 10.00	$ 156.00	-4.00%	-47.10%

Upside Potential [%]	Downside Protect. [%]	Trade ROO Premium [$]	Trade Upside Premium [$]	Total Capital Invested [$]
6.67%	0.00%	$ (600.00)	$ 1,000.00	$ 15,000.00

Figure 50: UTHR: Rolled-Out-And-Up-Trade Initial Returns

The spreadsheet shows an option debit of 4.00% ($6.00) but a share unrealized credit of $10.00 (6.67%) as long as share value remains above the (now) ITM $160.00 strike. The maximum return for the next contract month is 2.67% (6.67% – 4.00%).

Discussion

When our covered call trades are rolled-out, we close the current month trade by entering the (now) ITM strike as the final share value thereby maximizing the trade as initially structured. We then enter the next month, post adjustment trade, using the previous strike as our cost-basis and the net option credit/debit with the new expiration date. This applies to rolling-out (to the ITM strike) and rolling out-and-up to ITM, ATM and OTM strikes.

*** See Appendix IV for detailed information on entering & calculating rolling-out trades.

Chapter 13

Rolling-Out-And-Up to an OTM Strike

What is rolling-out-and-up to an OTM strike?

When rolling our covered call writing trades out-and-up, we close the near-month in-the-money (ITM) call and sell a higher strike option in the next contract cycle. The new strike can be ITM, ATM or OTM as it relates to current market value of the underlying security. Rolling-out-and-up to an OTM strike is the most bullish alternative of these 3 *moneyness* choices. By using an OTM strike, we create the opportunity for 2 income streams in the same contract cycle with the same cash investment, one from option premium and the other from share appreciation from current market value up to the new OTM strike.

If using Monthly options, this becomes a 2-month trade as initially structured. The dilemma becomes how to enter these trades into our trading log when measuring monthly results (can be other time frames, as well). This article will use a real-life example with United Therapeutics Corp., Inc. (Nasdaq: UTHR).

When to consider rolling-out-and-up to an OTM strike

We use this exit strategy when the strike price is ITM as expiration approaches and the security still meets our system and initial return requirements, including no upcoming earnings report. We select an OTM strike for the next contract cycle when bullish on the overall market and chart technical indicators are bullish and confirming.

Real-life example with UTHR

- 2/22/2021: Buy 100 x UTHR at $155.90
- 2/22/2021: STO 1 x 3/21/2021 $150.00 call at $9.25
- 3/21/2021: UTHR trading at $163.22
- 3/21/2021: BTC the 3/21/2021 $150.00 call at $15.50
- 3/21/2021: STO the 4/18/2021 $165.00 call at $6.50

Initial trade entries

Stock Symbol	Industry	Entry Trade Date	ER Date	Ex-Div Date	Entry Trade Expiry Date	Entry Stock Price [$/sh]	Entry Call Strike Price [$]	Entry Call Option Premium [$/sh]	Number Of Shares [#]
UTHR	Healthcare	02/22/21	04/20/21	NA	03/21/21	$ 155.90	$ 150.00	$ 9.25	100

Figure 51: UTHR: Entering Our Initial Trade

Initial trade returns

OPENING TRADE						
Expected # Of Days In Trade [#]	Time-Value Per-Share [$/sh]	Intrinsic-Value Per-Share [$/sh]	Upside Value Per-Share [$/sh]	Breakeven Value Per-Share [$/sh]	Return On Option ROO [%]	Return On Option ROO Annual'zd [%]
28	$ 3.35	$ 5.90	$ -	$ 146.65	2.23%	29.11%

Upside Potential [%]	Downside Protect. [%]	Trade ROO Premium [$]	Trade Upside Premium [$]	Total Capital Invested [$]
0.00%	3.78%	$ 335.00	$ -	$ 15,000.00

Figure 52: UTHR: Initial Trade Returns

The spreadsheet shows an initial time-value return of 2.23%, 29.11% annualized based on a 28-day trade, with 3.78% downside protection of that initial profit. The breakeven price point is $146.65.

How to manage these situations

Since the strike is ITM as expiration approaches, the initial trade return is maximized. We enter the final stock value as the ITM strike because that is what the shares are, in fact, worth due to our contract obligation to sell at that price. We, then, *enter the rolling aspect of the trade into the next contract cycle, using the initial strike as share value and the buy-to-close and sell-to-open rolling premiums as the net option premium for the next contract cycle.* This can result in a net credit or debit.

Trade adjustment entries

Stock Symbol	Exit Strategy Selected	Adjust. Trade Date	Adjust. Expiry Date	BTC Entry Option Price [$/Sh]	STO Entry #2 Strike Price [$]	STO Entry #2 Option Premium [$/Sh]	Final Stock Sale Price If Sold [$/Sh]	Final Unsold Stock Price [$/Sh]
UTHR	Roll-Out-and-Up							$ 150.00

Figure 53: UTHR: Trade Adjustments Prior to Rolling

Shares are valued at $150.00, the original strike price prior to rolling out-and-up.

Final calculations

Final Net Option Profit/Loss [$/Sh]	Final Net Option Profit/Loss [$]	Final Net Option Return [%]	Realized Final Stock Profit/Loss per share [$/Sh]	Realized Final $ Total Stock Profit/Loss [$]	Realized Final Stock Profit/Loss [%]	Unrealized Final Stock Profit/Loss [$/Sh]	Unrealized Final Stock $ Total Stock Profit/Loss [$]	Unreal. Final Stock % Total Stock Profit/Loss [%]
$ 9.25	$ 925.00	5.93%	$ -	$ -	-	$ (5.90)	$ (590.00)	-3.78%

FINAL RESULT	
Combined Final Trade Total Profit/Loss [$]	Combined Final Trade Total Profit/Loss [%]
$ 335.00	2.15%

Figure 54: UTHR: Final Results Prior to Rolling

The final pre-roll return is 2.15%. This includes an option credit of $925.00 (5.93%) and an unrealized stock debit of $590.00 (-3.78%) on an original cost-basis of $155.90. *Note that when we calculate initial calculations, we deduct intrinsic-value for ITM strikes as our cost-basis. When we calculate final returns, we use the original cost of the shares for ITM strikes, the same as we use for ATM and OTM strikes. The reason is that when we calculate initial returns, we use only the time-value component of the ITM premium but when we calculate final results, we use the entire ITM premium (time-value + intrinsic-value). This explains the slight difference between the initial returns (2.23%) and the final pre-roll return (2.15%).*

Entering the rolled-out trades into the next contract cycle

Stock Symbol	Industry	Entry Trade Date	ER Date	Ex-Div Date	Entry Trade Expiry Date	Entry Stock Price [$/sh]	Entry Call Strike Price [$]	Entry Call Option Premium [$/sh]	Number Of Shares [#]
UTHR	Healthcare	03/21/21	04/20/21	NA	04/18/21	$ 150.00	$ 165.00	$ (9.00)	100

Figure 55: UTHR: Entering the Roll-Out-And-Up Trade in the Next Contract Cycle

The stock value is the price of the stock based on our previous contract obligation to sell at $150.00. The option credit/debit (debit, in this case) is the cost-to-close the previous $150.00 strike ($15.50) and the premium received by selling the OTM $165.00 strike ($6.50). This results in an option net debit of $9.00. This data is based on current market value of $163.22.

Initial next contract returns after rolling-out-and-up into the next contract cycle

OPENING TRADE						
Expected # Of Days In Trade [#]	Time-Value Per-Share [$/sh]	Intrinsic-Value Per-Share [$/sh]	Upside Value Per-Share [$/sh]	Breakeven Value Per-Share [$/sh]	Return On Option ROO [%]	Return On Option ROO Annual'zd [%]
29	$ (9.00)	$ -	$ 15.00	$ 159.00	-6.00%	-75.52%

Upside Potential [%]	Downside Protect. [%]	Trade ROO Premium [$]	Trade Upside Premium [$]	Total Capital Invested [$]
10.00%	0.00%	$ (900.00)	$ 1,500.00	$ 15,000.00

Figure 56: UTHR: Next Month Initial Calculations

The spreadsheet shows an option debit of 6.00% but a share credit of up to 10.00% if share value moves up to or beyond the $165.00 OTM strike. It is currently trading at $163.22. The maximum return for the next contract month is 4.00% (10.00% - 6.00%).

Discussion

When rolling our covered call trades, we close the current month trade by entering the (now) ITM strike as the final share value thereby maximizing the trade as initially structured. We, then, enter the next month, post adjustment trade using the previous strike as our cost-basis and the net option credit/debit with the new strike and expiration date. This applies to rolling-out-and-up to ITM, ATM and OTM strikes.

*** See Appendix IV for detailed information on entering & calculating rolling-out trades.

Chapter 14

Using Multiple Exit Strategies in the Same Contract Cycle

What are multiple exit strategies?

These are situations where multiple exit strategy opportunities present *in the same contract month*. In this Select Sector SPDR Utilities (NYSE: XLU) example, we will use the *20% guideline* to close the original trade and setup a 2nd call sale in the same contract cycle, thereby *hitting a double*. This process is repeated resulting in *hitting a triple* or 3 income streams in the same contract cycle.

When to consider using multiple exit strategies

After we have executed one exit strategy opportunity, we are always alert for additional adjustment situations. After selling a second call in the same contract cycle, we always enter our 20%/10% BTC limit orders creating opportunities for additional exit strategy implementations.

What is the 20% guideline?

This guideline gives us a parameter that assists us in determining when to close our short call position should share value decline significantly in the first 2 weeks of a 4-week contract or the first 3 weeks of a 5-week contract. When share value falls substantially causing call value to decline, we should consider closing the short call position retaining

80% of the original premium profit and then deciding on our next maneuver. In the last 2 weeks of a contract, we change the 20% guideline to a 10% guideline.

What is hitting a double?

In the case of *hitting a double*, we wait for share value to recover and then re-sell the same option on the same underlying security with the same contract expiration. In our BCI community, if we can repeat this process a second time in the same contract cycle, we can refer to it as *hitting a triple*. This action will create an opportunity to generate additional income streams in the same contract cycle with a similar cash investment.

Real-life example with XLU

- 4/19/2021: Buy 100 x XLU at $67.05
- 4/19/2021: STO 1 x May 21, 2021 $68.00 calls at $0.66
- 4/28/2021: BTC 1 x May 21, 2021 $68.00 calls at $0.15 (20% guideline)
- 5/3/2021: STO 1 x May 21, 2021 $68.00 calls at $0.62 (that's our "double")
- 5/5/2021: BTC 1 x May 21, 2021 $68.00 calls at $0.12 (20% guideline)
- 5/10/2021: STO 1 x May 21, 2021 $68.00 calls at $0.33 (that's our "triple")
- 5/10/2021: *Set* a BTC limit order at $0.03 (10% guideline)

Graphic representation of the XLU triple

Figure 57: Hitting a Triple with 2 Classic V-Shaped Chart Patterns

Initial trade entries

Stock Symbol	Industry	Entry Trade Date	ER Date	Ex-Div Date	Entry Trade Expiry Date	Entry Stock Price [$/sh]	Entry Call Strike Price [$]	Entry Call Option Premium [$/sh]	Number Of Shares [#]
XLU	Utilities	04/19/21	NA	06/20/21	05/21/21	$ 67.05	$ 68.00	$ 0.66	100

Figure 58: XLU: Initial Trade Entries

Initial trade calculations and the 20% guideline

OPENING TRADE								
Expected # Of Days In Trade [#]	Time-Value Per-Share [$/sh]	Intrinsic-Value Per-Share [$/sh]	Upside Value Per-Share [$/sh]	Breakeve n Value Per-Share [$/sh]	Return On Option ROO [%]	Return On Option ROO Annual'zd [%]	Upside Potential [%]	Downside Protect. [%]
33	$ 0.66	$ -	$ 0.95	$ 66.39	0.98%	10.89%	1.42%	0.00%
Trade ROO Premium [$]	Trade Upside Premium [$]	Total Capital Invested [$]	20% Option Exit Guideline [$]	10% Option Exit Guideline [$]	7% Stock Exit Guideline [$]			
$ 66.00	$ 95.00	$ 6,705.00	$ 0.13	$ 0.07	$ 62.36			

Figure 59: XLU: Initial Trade Returns Showing the 20% Guideline

The initial return on the option (ROO) is a 33-day return of 0.98%, 10.89% annualized. The upside potential is 1.42% and the breakeven price point is $66.39 (yellow cell).

The 20% guideline sets a threshold price to buy-to-close the short call at $0.13 or lower. This is an approximate threshold price point and that is why it is referenced as a *guideline.* Note that $6,705.00 per-contract represented the cash invested in the trade.

How to manage these situations

After entering the initial trade, set a buy-to-close (BTC) limit order good-until-cancelled (GTC) at $0.13. If the platform only accepts these orders in $0.05 increments, set the BTC GTC limit order at $0.15.

Enter the date the short call is closed based on the 20% guideline, the BTC and STO premiums and original value of the stock.

Trade adjustment entries

Stock Symbol	Exit Strategy Selected	Adjust. Trade Date	Adjust. Expiry Date	BTC Entry Option Price [$/Sh]	STO Entry #2 Strike Price [$]	STO Entry #2 Option Premium [$/Sh]	Final Stock Sale Price If Sold [$/Sh]	Final Unsold Stock Price [$/Sh]
XLU	Hit Double/Keep Stock	04/28/21		$ 0.15	$ 68.00	$ 0.62		$ 67.05

Figure 60: XLU: Hitting a Double Adjustments

The BTC ($0.15) and STO ($0.62) trades are entered and the share price cost-basis remains the original $67.05.

Initial trade final calculations

Final Net Option Profit/Loss [$/Sh]	Final Net Option Profit/Loss [$]	Final Net Option Return [%]	Realized Final Stock Profit/Loss per share [$/Sh]	Realized Final $ Total Stock Profit/Loss [$]	Realized Final Stock Profit/Loss [%]	Unrealized Final Stock Profit/Loss [$/Sh]	Unrealized Final Stock $ Total Stock Profit/Loss [$]	Unreal. Final Stock % Total Stock Profit/Loss [%]
$ 1.13	$ 113.00	1.69%	$ -	$ -	-	$ -	$ -	0.00%

FINAL RESULT	
Combined Final Trade Total Profit/Loss [$]	Combined Final Trade Total Profit/Loss [%]
$ 113.00	1.69%

Figure 61: XLU: Final Results After Hitting a Double

The Trade Management Calculator shows a return of $113.00 per-contract which represents a 1.69% mid-contract return, up from the pre-adjustment return of 0.98% and we're not done yet.

We enter another 20% BTC GTC limit order on the last call sale at $0.12 (20% of $0.62) which was executed on 5/5/2021. A 3rd call was sold at $0.33 (that's the *triple*). These last 2 trades are *entered into the spreadsheet as another trade in the same contract month.*

Entering the 2nd trade in the same contract month (second income stream)

Since we still own the 100 shares of XLU, no additional cash is added to the second trade.

Stock Symbol	Industry	Entry Trade Date	ER Date	Ex-Div Date	Entry Trade Expiry Date	Entry Stock Price [$/sh]	Entry Call Strike Price [$]	Entry Call Option Premium [$/sh]	Number Of Shares [#]
XLU	Utilities	04/19/21	NA	06/20/01	05/21/21	$ 67.05	$ 68.00	$ 0.66	100
TMUS	Telecom	05/18/20	06/20/20	06/26/20	06/19/20	$ 79.59	$ 77.50	$ 4.25	100
DEF		01/24/22			03/18/22	$ 48.00	$ 45.00	$ 5.00	100
GHI		01/24/22			03/18/22	$ 48.00	$ 50.00	$ 1.50	100
JKL		01/24/22			03/18/22	$ 48.00	$ 50.00	$ 1.50	100
MNO		01/24/22			03/18/22	$ 48.00	$ 45.00	$ 5.00	100
PQR		01/24/22			03/18/22	$ 48.00	$ 45.00	$ 5.00	100
STU		01/24/22			03/18/22	$ 48.00	$ 45.00	$ 5.00	100
VWY		01/24/22			03/18/22	$ 48.00	$ 50.00	$ 1.50	100
ZAB		01/24/22			03/18/22	$ 48.00	$ 45.00	$ 5.00	100
XLU		05/10/21			05/21/21	$ 67.05	$ 68.00	$ 0.21	100

Figure 62: XLU: Entering the 2nd Post-Adjusted Trade

The brown-highlighted row shows the initial trade entries and the green-highlighted row reflects the second trade. Note that the entry call premium is $0.21, which represents ($0.33 - $0.12), the BTC and STO premiums used to *hit a triple.*

Total capital invested correction needed after second trade entry

Return On Option ROO [%]	Return On Option ROO Annual'zd [%]	Upside Potential [%]	Down Protect. [%]	Trade ROO Premium [$]	Trade Upside Premium [$]	Total Capital Invested [$]
0.98%	10.89%	1.42%	0.00%	$ 66.00	$ 95.00	$ 6,705.00
2.79%	30.83%	0.00%	2.63%	$ 216.00	$ -	$ 7,750.00
4.44%	30.04%	0.00%	6.25%	$ 200.00	$ -	$ 4,500.00
3.13%	21.12%	4.17%	0.00%	$ 150.00	$ 200.00	$ 4,800.00
3.13%	21.12%	4.17%	0.00%	$ 150.00	$ 200.00	$ 4,800.00
4.44%	30.04%	0.00%	6.25%	$ 200.00	$ -	$ 4,500.00
4.44%	30.04%	0.00%	6.25%	$ 200.00	$ -	$ 4,500.00
4.44%	30.04%	0.00%	6.25%	$ 200.00	$ -	$ 4,500.00
3.13%	21.12%	4.17%	0.00%	$ 150.00	$ 200.00	$ 4,800.00
4.44%	30.04%	0.00%	6.25%	$ 200.00	$ -	$ 4,500.00
0.31%	9.53%	1.42%	0.00%	$ 21.00	$ 95.00	$ 6,705.00

Figure 63: XLU: Redundancy in Total Capital Invested

The spreadsheet shows an additional capital investment of $6,705.00, when, in reality, it is the same cash investment from the original purchase of the shares. This is misleading because the same cash investment is used in the second trade and will skew the final % portfolio returns.

How to correct total cash invested after entering a second trade in the same contract cycle with the same cash investment

We scroll down and enter a capital adjustment of -$6,705.00 into the *capital adjustment section* of the spreadsheet. Enter a negative total capital invested at the bottom of Column W (blue cell under Column W) and the corresponding ticker symbol is noted in column A (blue cell). The proper Total

Capital Invested will now be calculated for our total portfolio capital invested (red arrow).

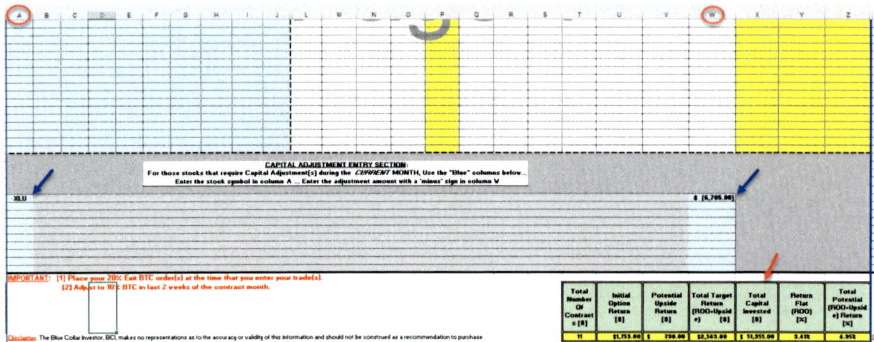

Figure 64: Capital Adjustment Section of the BCI Trade Management Calculator

Close-up views

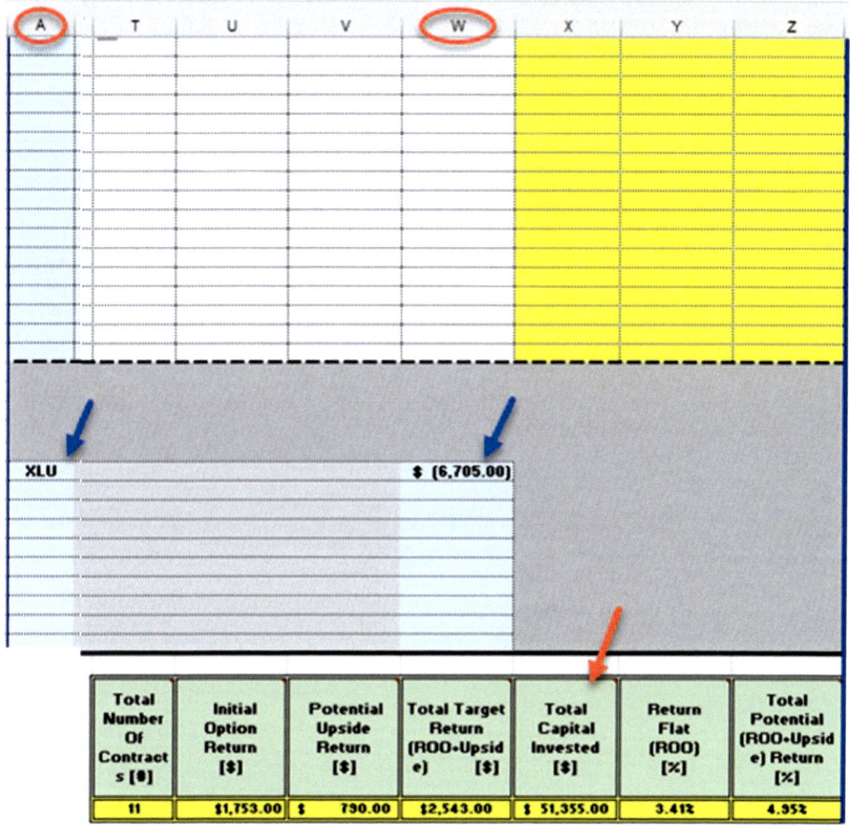

Figure 65: XLU: Capital Adjustment Entries

Discussion

When using multiple exit strategies in the same contract cycle, we must first close the initial adjusted trade. The second-income trade is entered in another row and a capital adjustment subtraction is entered in Column W (Total Capital Invested) directly below the 2nd trade calculations. This will maintain the accuracy of the total capital invested.

Section II: Exit Strategies for Selling Cash-Secured Puts

Chapter 15

What is Selling Cash-Secured Puts?

Introduction

Selling cash-secured puts is a low-risk investment strategy that generates cash-flow by undertaking a contractual obligation to purchase shares at the strike price by the expiration date. We, the option-sellers, determine the price we are willing to pay for the shares as well as the contract expiration date. In return for undertaking this obligation, we are paid a cash premium.

The broker will require us to place the cash into our brokerage account to *secure* that put in the event the option is exercised by the option holder. The required amount is the put strike minus the put premium times the number of underlying shares.

To sum up: we place an appropriate amount of cash into our brokerage account and sell the corresponding put which gives the buyer (option holder) the right, but not the obligation, to sell their shares to us (the option sellers) at a certain price (called the *strike price*) by a certain date (known as the *expiration date*). In return for undertaking this obligation we receive a cash premium that the market determines.

Preview example

Let's start with a *basic hypothetical example* of selling a cash-secured put. Assume stock BCI is currently trading at $75.00 and we want to sell, or *write* 1 x $72.50 BCI put option, which is valued at $2.00 ($200.00 per-contract) and has a 1-month expiration. We deposit $7,250.00 less the $200.00 put premium into our brokerage cash account (per 100 shares of obligation), and sell that put option for $200.00 (per 100 shares of obligation).

The amount we are investing or risking is $7,250.00 - $200.00 = $7,050.00. We are now be obligated to buy 100 shares of BCI at $72.50 per share from the put buyer *if* the put buyer chooses to exercise the put option. The $200.00 premium, however, is ours to keep no matter what transpires. Let's go over some key concepts that appear in this hypothetical:

- *1 Option = 100 Shares of Stock:* In this example, we sold 1 BCI put option. In other words, we sold some unknown person the right, but not the obligation, to sell 100 shares of BCI to us on or before the option's one-month expiration date (usually the 3rd Friday of the month at 4 PM ET). If we sold 5 BCI put options, we would have sold some unknown person the right, but not the obligation, to sell us 500 shares of BCI.

- *Strike Price = $72.50:* We sold some unknown person the right, but not the obligation, to sell us 100 shares of BCI at $72.50 per share, which is the strike price of the option. Because the strike price ($72.50) was lower than the stock price of BCI ($75.00) at the time of the sale, we sold an *out-of-the-money* put option. *Out-of-the money put strikes are favored in our BCI methodology.*

- *$7,050.00 Deposit Secured Our Put Option Sale:* As a result of the sale of our put option, we *may* be required to buy BCI stock at $72.50 per share. Here, we sold 1 option contract, which equals 100 shares of BCI. Thus, depositing $7,050.00 (100 shares of BCI x $72.50/BCI share, less the $2.00 put premium) into our brokerage account renders the sale of our put option *cash-secured.* In other words, this deposit ensures that we have enough money in our brokerage account in the event the put buyer *exercises* his right to sell us 100 shares of BCI at $72.50 (i.e., in the event we are forced to buy 100 shares of BCI).

- *$2.00 = Our Options Premium:* In exchange for giving some unknown person (the put buyer) the right to sell us 100 shares of BCI stock at $72.50, we get paid in the form of a *premium.* In this example, our premium is $2.00 per share. Because each options contract equals 100 shares of stock, our premium is $200.00 per-contract. This $200.00 is ours to keep no matter what transpires before expiration (the end of the contract).

- *Unexercised Profit:* Our initial profit from the put sale is equal to our premium ($200.00) divided by the amount of money we need to set aside to secure the sale of the put option ($7,250.00 - $200.00). In other words, here our unexercised profit was $200/$7,050 = 2.8% (less small trading commissions). A 2.8% profit annualizes to a 34% return on our investment.

Two Primary Outcomes

As demonstrated in the preview example, when we sell cash-secured puts we are obligated to have a sufficient amount of cash in our brokerage account to buy the underlying shares of stock at the strike price. However, purchasing the underlying shares at the strike price is only one of two possible scenarios. Referring to our preview example, let's briefly go over the two primary outcomes that can result when we sell cash-secured puts:

1- If the stock price of BCI remains above the strike price of the put option we sold ($72.50) through expiration, the option buyer (holder) is not going to elect to exercise the option and sell 100 shares of BCI to us at a price lower than the current market value.
Put yourself in the position of the options holder (the unknown person that buys the put option from us) for a moment. The put holder purchased the right, but not the obligation, to sell 100 shares of BCI at $72.50 per share. Assume this put option expires in one month. If, at the end of that one-month expiration time period, BCI stock is trading at a price above

$72.50, why would the put holder exercise his right to sell BCI stock at $72.50 when he can sell at a price above $72.50? He wouldn't. In this scenario, the option will expire worthless, and we pocket $200.00 (the premium) with no further obligation. As the put sellers, we have generated a 2.8%, one-month return ($200.00/$7,050.00), and that cash is now free to secure the sale of another put option that expires in the next contract cycle.

2- In the second possible primary outcome, the stock price of BCI is trading at a price below the $72.50 strike price at the time the put option is about to expire. Here, if we take no exit strategy action, the option will be exercised and the shares of BCI will be sold to us at the strike price ($72.50 per share). Again, put yourself in the position of the put holder for a moment. If, at the time the put option is set to expire, BCI stock is trading at $70.00, and the put holder has the right to sell shares of BCI stock at $72.50, why wouldn't the put holder exercise her right to sell BCI stock at $72.50 per share? She would. In this scenario, the cash we (as put sellers) previously deposited into our brokerage account ($7,050.00 + the $200.00 put premium) is used to purchase the underlying shares of BCI that were *put* or sold to us.

Our break-even point, also referred to as our *cost-basis*, is now $70.50 ($72.50 per share we paid for BCI stock less the $2.00 per share put premium we received from the original sale of the put option). At this point, we now own 100 shares of BCI stock and have the opportunity to take one of the following paths:

- Sell the 100 shares of BCI stock for a capital gain or loss
- Hold the 100 shares of BCI stock for the long term
- Write a covered call on the stock (giving the call option buyer the right to buy these shares from us) to generate additional income. This approach is known as the *PCP (put-call-put) strategy* in the BCI community (also known as the *wheel strategy*) and will be detailed in Chapter 27

Summary

Selling cash-secured puts is a low-risk option-selling strategy where we undertake the contractual obligation to buy shares at the strike price by the expiration date. In return, we receive a cash premium. All stock (ETFs, as well) and option selections should be based on our rigorous system requirements. Once we enter our put-selling trades, we move immediately into position management mode.

This section will now focus on the extensive exit strategy arsenal we have available to mitigate losses, enhance gains and even turn losses into gains after entering our cash-secured put trades.

Chapter 16

3% Guideline

When we sell cash-secured puts, we must use all 3 of our required skills: stock (or ETF) selection, option selection and position management. Once we have selected an elite-performing security, we then choose an out-of-the-money (OTM) put strike that meets our initial time-value return goal range (2% – 4% per-month, for me). Without exit strategies, our maximum return is the put premium and that profit is realized as long as share price does not decline below the OTM put strike. But, what do we do if share value does decline below that put strike despite our rigorous screening process? Enter our *3% guideline* for selling cash-secured puts.

What is the 3% guideline?

This guideline gives us a parameter that assists us in determining when to close our short put position should share value decline significantly. When share value drops more than 3% below the OTM put strike, we should consider closing the short put position. Most of the time, this will result in a trade loss. The cash used to secure that original put trade can then be used to initiate a new put sale, in the same contract cycle, with a different underlying to recover some or all of those losses. Rolling-down, another potential exit strategy choice, will be addressed in Chapter 22.

This guideline was developed based on an initial monthly time-value return goal range of 2% - 4%. For investors who use different ranges, that guideline can be adjusted. For weekly options, I would consider closing if the share price drops below the OTM put strike.

When to consider using the 3% guideline

When share price drops more than 3% below the OTM put strike and we don't want to take possession of the shares, this is a reasonable threshold to use, assuming the initial time-value return goal range of 2% - 4%.

Real-life example with Nvidia Corp. (Nasdaq: NVDA)

- 8/20/2021: NVDA trading at $208.16
- 8/20/2021: STO 1 x 9/24/2021 $200.00 put at $5.65
- 9/10/2021: NVDA trading at $194.00 (3% guideline)
- 9/10/2-21: Cost-to-close the $200.00, now ITM, put is $7.50

Initial trade entries

Stock Symbol	Industry	Entry Trade Date	ER Date	Ex Div Date	Entry Trade Expiry Date	Entry Stock Price [$/sh]	Entry Put Strike Price [$]	Entry Put Option Price [$/sh]	# Shares
NVDA	Computer	8/20/21	11/18/21	12/17/21	09/24/21	$ 208.16	$ 200.00	$ 5.65	100

Figure 66: NVDA: Entering Our Initial Trade

Initial trade returns and the 3% guideline

OPENING TRADE							
Expected # Of Days In Trade [#]	Time Value [$/sh]	Put Premium Collected Per Contract [$]	Cash Req/Cont [$]	Breakeve n [$/sh]	Return On Option ROO [%]	Return On Option ROO Annual'zd [%]	ROO Premium [$]
36	$ 5.65	$ 565.00	$ 19,435.00	$ 194.35	2.91%	29.48%	$ 565.00

Purchase Discount If Exercised [%]	Stock Cost/Share If Exercised [$/sh]	Total Capital Invested [$]	3% Stock Exit Guideline [$]	20% Optn Exit Guideline [$]	10% Optn Exit Guideline [$]
6.63%	$ 194.35	$ 19,435.00	$ 194.00	$ 1.13	$ 0.57

Figure 67: NVDA: Initials Trade Returns Showing the 3% Guideline

The initial return on the option is 2.91%, 29.48% annualized based on a 36-day trade. If the put is exercised, shares are purchased at a 6.63% discount from the original price of NVDA when the put sale was initiated. The breakeven price point is $194.35.

What is our loss if NVDA drops below the $194.00 3% guideline price point?

Is it $0.35 per-share ($194.35 BE – $194.00 put strike)?

If the shares are put to us at the put strike of $200.00 and NVDA is trading at $194.00, we are losing $0.35 per-share. Do we want to wait until expiration on this declining security? Utilizing the 3% guideline will result in a debit but avoid catastrophic losses if share value continues to decline.

Is it greater than $0.35 per-share?

If we are forced to close the short put due to breach of the 3% threshold, we will be losing more than $0.35 per-share. This is because we have to spend money to close the short put (buy-to-close or BTC). That loss will be represented by the following formula:

[$5.65 – (cost-to-close the short put)]

There are 2 Greek factors at work that will determine the cost-to-close (CTC) the short put:

- *Delta:* Share decline increases the value of the put making it more expensive to buy back
- *Theta:* As time progresses, the time-value erosion effect of Theta will cause put value to decline

Overall, we should expect the CTC to be greater than the initial put premium resulting in a trade loss.

How to manage our 3% guideline adjustments

We enter the date that we are closing the short put, the BTC cost and the current value of the shares at the time of the contract adjustment. The purpose of entering share value is to allow us to review and analyze trades after their executions. It's a learning opportunity.

Trade adjustment entries

Stock Symbol	Exit Strategy Selected	Adjust. Trade Date	Adjust. Expiry Date	BTC Entry Option Price [$/Sh]	STO Entry #2 Strike Price [$/Sh]	STO Entry #2 Option Premium [$/Sh]	Current Stock Price Basis [$]	Price of Stock At Time of Exercise [$]
NVDA	3% Stock Price Decline Exit	09/10/21		$ 7.50			$ 194.00	

Figure 68: NVDA: 3% Guideline Adjustments

Final calculations

Final Net Option Profit/Loss [$/Sh]	Final Net Option Profit/Loss [$]	Final Net Option Return [%]	Unrealized Final Stock Profit/Loss [$]	Unrealized Final Stock $ Total Stock Profit/Loss [$]	Unreal. Final Stock % Total Stock Profit/Loss [%]
$ (1.85)	$ (185.00)	-0.95%	$ -	$ -	0.00%

FINAL RESULT	
Combined Final Trade Total Profit/Loss [$]	Combined Final Trade Total Profit/Loss [%]
$ (185.00)	-0.95%

Figure 69: NVDA: Final Results After 3% Guideline Execution

The spreadsheet shows a loss of $185.00 per-contract or 0.95% based on the initial investment.

Discussion

The 3% guideline is used to mitigate losses and potential greater depreciation. In the case of NVDA, if share price drops from $208.16 to $194.00 (3% guideline), we have a problem and must take action. The spreadsheet shows the BE price point to be $194.35 resulting in a loss of $0.35 per-share if shares are *put* to us at $194.00.

Breakeven = [put strike – put premium].

I, generally, wait for share price decline of > 3% by the end of a trading day and close the following morning if the 3% status is still in place.

This stat does not include any exit strategy executions. If we bought back the put option as share price declined, the loss would be ($5.65 – cost-to-close the $200.00 put). This would result in a loss greater than $0.35 per-share but would also mitigate additional losses on a security that has declined in value substantially in this example. *Not all trades will be winners. Our job, as CEOs of our own money, is to mitigate losses and enhance gains.*

Chapter 17

10% Guideline

What is the 10% guideline?

This guideline gives us a parameter that assists us in determining when to close our short put position should share value accelerate significantly in the last 2 weeks of a monthly contract.

When to consider the 10% guideline

When share value rises substantially causing put value to decline, we should consider closing the short put position retaining 90% of the original premium profit and moving to a new cash-secured put trade with a different underlying security. *Share value and put value are inversely related*. This action will create an opportunity to generate an additional income stream in the same contract cycle with the same cash investment. If we sold a put option for $2.00, we would immediately enter a BTC GTC limit order at $0.20 in the last 2 weeks of a monthly contract.

Real-life example with NVDA

- 8/20/2021: NVDA trading at $208.16
- 8/20/2021: STO the 9/24/2021 $200.00 put at $5.65
- 9/7/2021: NVDA trading at $215.23
- 9/7/2021: CTC the $200.00 put is $0.52

Initial trade entries

Stock Symbol	Industry	Entry Trade Date	ER Date	Ex Div Date	Entry Trade Expiry Date	Entry Stock Price [$/sh]	Entry Put Strike Price [$]	Entry Put Option Price [$/sh]	# Shares
NVDA	Computer	8/20/21	11/18/21	12/17/21	09/24/21	$ 208.16	$ 200.00	$ 5.65	100

Figure 70: NVDA: Entering Our Initial Trade

Initial trade returns and the 10% guideline

OPENING TRADE								
Expected # Of Days In Trade [#]	Time Value [$/sh]	Put Premium Collected Per Contract [$]	Cash Req/Cont [$]	Breakeven [$/sh]	Return On Option ROO [%]	Return On Option ROO Annual'zd [%]	ROO Premium [$]	Purchase Discount If Exercised [%]
36	$ 5.65	$ 565.00	$ 19,435.00	$ 194.35	2.91%	29.48%	$ 565.00	6.63%

Stock Cost/Share If Exercised [$/sh]	Total Capital Invested [$]	3% Stock Exit Guideline [$]	20% Optn Exit Guideline [$]	10% Optn Exit Guideline [$]
$ 194.35	$ 19,435.00	$ 194.00	$ 1.13	$ 0.57

Figure 71: NVDA: Initial Returns and the 10% Guideline

The initial return on the option (ROO) is a 36-day return of 2.91%, 29.48% annualized based on a 36-day trade. If the put option is exercised, the purchase discount is 6.63%. The 10% guideline sets a threshold price to buy-to-close the short put at $0.57 or lower.

How to manage the 10% guideline exit strategy

After entering the initial monthly trade, set a buy-to-close (BTC) limit order good-until-cancelled (GTC) at $0.57 or lower in the last 2 weeks of a monthly contract. If the platform only accepts these orders in $0.05 increments, set the BTC GTC limit order at $0.55.

We enter the date of the trade adjustment, the BTC premium and current price of stock when the short put was closed.

Trade adjustment entries

Stock Symbol	Exit Strategy Selected	Adjust. Trade Date	Adjust. Expiry Date	BTC Entry Option Price [$/Sh]	STO Entry #2 Strike Price [$/Sh]	STO Entry #2 Option Premium [$/Sh]	Current Stock Price Basis [$]	Price of Stock At Time of Exercise [$]
NVDA	10% Option Buy-Back Gdln	09/07/21		$ 0.52			$ 215.23	

Figure 72: NVDA: 10% Guideline Adjustments

Final calculations

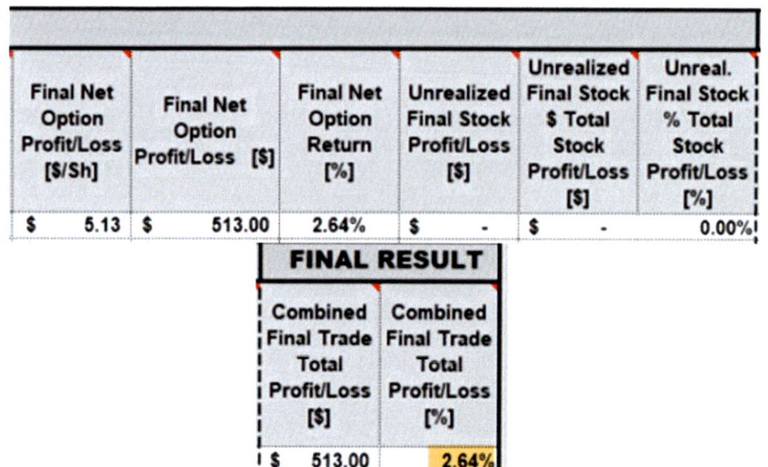

Final Net Option Profit/Loss [$/Sh]	Final Net Option Profit/Loss [$]	Final Net Option Return [%]	Unrealized Final Stock Profit/Loss [$]	Unrealized Final Stock $ Total Stock Profit/Loss [$]	Unreal. Final Stock % Total Stock Profit/Loss [%]
$ 5.13	$ 513.00	2.64%	$ -	$ -	0.00%

FINAL RESULT

Combined Final Trade Total Profit/Loss [$]	Combined Final Trade Total Profit/Loss [%]
$ 513.00	2.64%

Figure 73: NVDA: Final Results After 0% Guideline Adjustments

The realized option profit moved down slightly from the initial 2.91% to the final 2.64%, having retained 90% of the original option profit. We now have the cash freed up to enter a new position and generate a second income stream in the same contract cycle with the same cash investment.

Discussion

The 10% guideline is used when share value increases significantly causing put value to decline. This creates an opportunity to generate a 2nd income stream, or multiple income streams, in the same contract cycle by closing the initial short put when the threshold is reached. We use a different underlying security to avoid profit-taking of the recently appreciated security.

Chapter 18

20% Guideline

What is the 20% guideline?

This guideline gives us a parameter that assists us in determining when to close our short put position should share value accelerate significantly in the first 2 weeks of a 4-week contract or the first 3 weeks of a 5-week contract.

When to consider the 20% guideline

When share value rises substantially causing put value to decline, we should consider closing the short put position retaining 80% of the original premium profit and moving to a new cash-secured put trade with a different underlying security and the same expiration date. This action will create an opportunity to generate an additional income stream in the same contract cycle with the same cash investment. If we sold a put option for $2.00, we would immediately enter a BTC GTC limit order at $0.40 in the first 2 weeks of a 4-week contract or the first 3 weeks of a 5-week contract.

Real-life example with NVDA

- 8/20/2021: NVDA trading at $208.16
- 8/20/2021: STO the 9/24/2021 $200.00 put at $5.65
- 8/27/2021: NVDA trading at $216.23
- 8/27/2021: CTC the $200.00 put is $1.10

Initial trade entries

Stock Symbol	Industry	Entry Trade Date	ER Date	Ex Div Date	Entry Trade Expiry Date	Entry Stock Price [$/sh]	Entry Put Strike Price [$]	Entry Put Option Price [$/sh]	# Shares
NVDA	Computer	8/20/21	11/18/21	12/17/21	09/24/21	$ 208.16	$ 200.00	$ 5.65	100

Figure 74: NVDA: Entering Our Initial Trade

Initial trade returns showing the 20% guideline

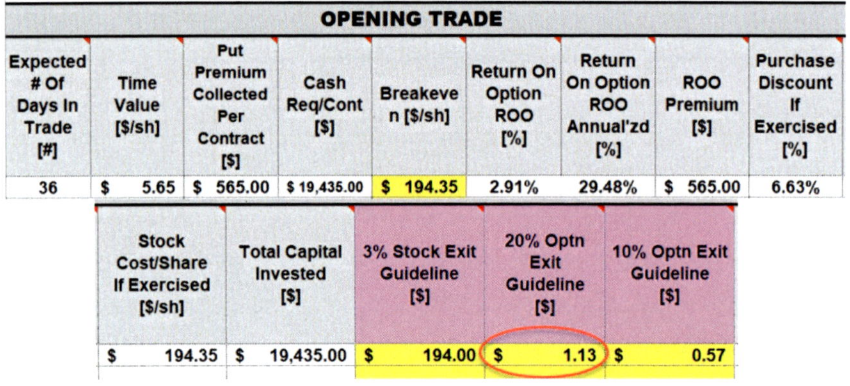

OPENING TRADE								
Expected # Of Days In Trade [#]	Time Value [$/sh]	Put Premium Collected Per Contract [$]	Cash Req/Cont [$]	Breakeven [$/sh]	Return On Option ROO [%]	Return On Option ROO Annual'zd [%]	ROO Premium [$]	Purchase Discount If Exercised [%]
36	$ 5.65	$ 565.00	$ 19,435.00	$ 194.35	2.91%	29.48%	$ 565.00	6.63%

Stock Cost/Share If Exercised [$/sh]	Total Capital Invested [$]	3% Stock Exit Guideline [$]	20% Optn Exit Guideline [$]	10% Optn Exit Guideline [$]
$ 194.35	$ 19,435.00	$ 194.00	$ 1.13	$ 0.57

Figure 75: NVDA: Initial Trade Returns and the 20% Guideline

The initial return on the option (ROO) is a 36-day return of 2.91%, 29.48% annualized based on a 36-day trade. If the put option is exercised, the purchase discount is 6.63%. The 20% guideline sets a threshold price to buy-to-close the short put at $1.13 or lower.

How to manage the 20% guideline exit strategy

After entering the initial monthly trade, set a buy-to-close (BTC) limit order good-until-cancelled (GTC) at $1.13 in the first 2 weeks of a 4-week monthly contract or in the first 3 weeks of a 5-week monthly contract. If the platform only accepts these orders in $0.05 increments, set the BTC GTC limit order at $1.15.

We enter the date of the trade adjustment, the BTC premium and current price of stock when the short put was closed.

Trade adjustment entries

				CLOSING TRADE				
Stock Symbol	Exit Strategy Selected	Adjust. Trade Date	Adjust. Expiry Date	BTC Entry Option Price [$/Sh]	STO Entry #2 Strike Price [$/Sh]	STO Entry #2 Option Premium [$/Sh]	Current Stock Price Basis [$]	Price of Stock At Time of Exercise [$]
NVDA	20% Option Buy-Back Gdln	08/27/21		$ 1.10			$ 216.23	

Figure 76: NVDA: 20% Guideline Adjustments

Final calculations

						FINAL RESULT	
Final Net Option Profit/Loss [$/Sh]	Final Net Option Profit/Loss [$]	Final Net Option Return [%]	Unrealized Final Stock Profit/Loss [$]	Unrealized Final Stock $ Total Stock Profit/Loss [$]	Unreal. Final Stock % Total Stock Profit/Loss [%]	Combined Final Trade Total Profit/Loss [$]	Combined Final Trade Total Profit/Loss [%]
$ 4.55	$ 455.00	2.34%	$ -	$ -	0.00%	$ 455.00	2.34%

Figure 77: NVDA: Final Results After 20% Guideline Adjustments

The realized option profit moved down slightly from the initial 2.91% to the final 2.34%, having retained 80% of the original option profit. We now have the cash freed up to enter a new position and generate a second income stream in the same contract with the same cash investment using a different underlying security.

Discussion

The 20% guideline is used when share value increases significantly causing put value to decline. This creates an opportunity to generate a 2nd income stream, or multiple income streams, in the same contract cycle by closing the initial short put when the threshold is reached. We use a different underlying security to avoid profit-taking of the recently appreciated security.

Chapter 19

Allowing Exercise

What is allowing exercise of an ITM put strike?

This is where we take no action as expiration approaches when the put strike is about to expire in-the-money (with intrinsic-value). The *Options Clearing Corporation (OCC)* will automatically exercise an option that is in-the-money by $0.01 or more, unless otherwise instructed by our broker. The shares will be put to us at the strike at a *cost-basis of the put-strike minus the original put premium.*

When to consider allowing exercise of an ITM strike?

We use this strategy approach when we want to take possession of the underlying shares. Our goal may have been to buy the security at a discount and retain in our longer-term buy-and-hold portfolio or to then sell a covered call option (*PCP or put-call-put strategy,* also known as the wheel strategy, discussed in Chapter 27). We will continue to use our NVDA example to highlight this strategy approach.

Real-life example with NVIDIA Corp. (Nasdaq: NVDA)

- 8/20/2021: NVDA trading at $208.16
- 8/20/2021: STO 1 x 9/24/2021 $200.00 put at $5.65
- 9/24/2021, NVDA is trading at $199.00, leaving the original short put strike ($200.00) in-the-money by $1.00

Initial trade entries

Stock Symbol	Industry	Entry Trade Date	ER Date	Ex Div Date	Entry Trade Expiry Date	Entry Stock Price [$/sh]	Entry Put Strike Price [$]	Entry Put Option Price [$/sh]	# Shares
NVDA	Computer	8/20/21	11/18/21	12/17/21	09/24/21	$ 208.16	$ 200.00	$ 5.65	100

Figure 78: NVDA: Entering Our Initial Trade

Initial trade returns

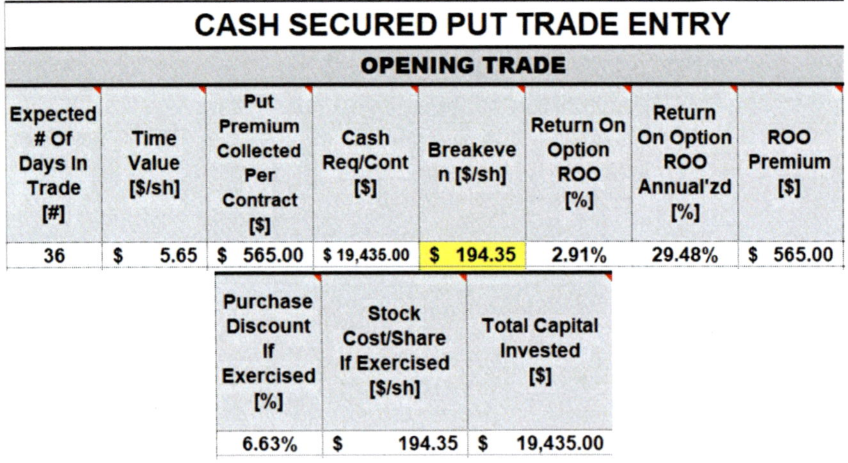

CASH SECURED PUT TRADE ENTRY

OPENING TRADE

Expected # Of Days In Trade [#]	Time Value [$/sh]	Put Premium Collected Per Contract [$]	Cash Req/Cont [$]	Breakeven [$/sh]	Return On Option ROO [%]	Return On Option ROO Annual'zd [%]	ROO Premium [$]
36	$ 5.65	$ 565.00	$ 19,435.00	$ 194.35	2.91%	29.48%	$ 565.00

Purchase Discount If Exercised [%]	Stock Cost/Share If Exercised [$/sh]	Total Capital Invested [$]
6.63%	$ 194.35	$ 19,435.00

Figure 79: NVDA: Initial Trade Returns

The Trade Management Calculator shows an initial return on the option of 2.91%, 29.48% annualized based on a 36-day trade. Should the option be exercised, the breakeven price point is $194.35 or a 6.63% discount from the original price of $208.16.

How to manage allowing exercise trades

The original put trade is considered closed on the expiration date by entering the current price of the stock at the time of exercise.

CLOSING TRADE								
Stock Symbol	Exit Strategy Selected	Adjust. Trade Date	Adjust. Expiry Date	BTC Entry Option Price [$/Sh]	STO Entry #2 Strike Price [$/Sh]	STO Entry #2 Option Premium [$/Sh]	Current Stock Price Basis [$]	Price of Stock At Time of Exercise [$]
NVDA	Allow Exercise	09/24/21						$ 199.00

Figure 80: NVDA: Allowing Exercise Adjustments

Final calculations after allowing exercise

Final Net Option Profit/Loss [$/Sh]	Final Net Option Profit/Loss [$]	Final Net Option Return [%]	Unrealized Final Stock Profit/Loss [$]	Unrealized Final Stock $ Total Stock Profit/Loss [$]	Unreal. Final Stock % Total Stock Profit/Loss [%]	Combined Final Trade Total Profit/Loss [$]	Combined Final Trade Total Profit/Loss [%]
$ 5.65	$ 565.00	2.91%	$ (1.00)	$ (100.00)	-0.50%	$ 465.00	2.39%

Figure 81: NVDA: Final results After Allowing Exercise

The spreadsheet will calculate the following:

- The final time-value option return of $5.65 per-share or 2.91% (green cells)
- An unrealized share loss of $1.00 per-share or 0.50% (brown cells)
- A final combined unrealized trade profit of $465.00 or 2.39% (yellow cells)

We now own the shares at a cost-basis of $194.35 ($200.00 - $5.65) with the stock trading at $199.00 and can retain in a longer-term buy-and-hold portfolio, sell the stock or write a covered call.

Discussion

We consider allowing exercise of an ITM put strike when the security still meets all system criteria, and we want to take possession of the shares. The cash generation process can continue by writing covered calls on these shares. See Chapter 27, The PCP Strategy, for more details on this strategy approach.

Chapter 20

Closing ITM Puts

What is closing ITM put strikes?

If a strike is in-the-money as expiration approaches, we may opt to close the position rather than roll the option or allow exercise. This may result in a net option credit or debit and will avoid exercise of the put option and having shares *put* to us.

When to consider closing an ITM strike?

Reasons to take this approach include:

- There is an upcoming earnings report in the next contract cycle
- The underlying security no longer meets our system requirements (fundamental, technical and common-sense screens)
- The rolling calculations do not meet our stated initial time-value return goal range

Difference between rolling and closing an existing ITM put strike as expiration approaches

When we roll the option, we BTC the near-term strike and STO the next contract same put strike. If we decide to close the ITM strike and simply exit the trade, we only close the current put trade and look to establish a new cash-secured put trade with a different security at the start of the next contract cycle. Let's use the same NVDA example but assume one of the factors exist that would eliminate rolling considerations.

Real-life example with Nvidia (Nasdaq: NVDA)

- 8/20/2021: NVDA trading at $208.16
- 8/20/2021: STO the 9/24/2021 $200.00 put at $5.65
- 9/24/2021, NVDA is trading at $199.00, leaving the original short put strike ($200.00) in-the-money).
- BTC cost is $1.10 ($1.00 of intrinsic-value and $0.10 of time-value)
- A decision is made to close and exit the trade rather than roll the trade

Initial trade entries

Stock Symbol	Industry	Entry Trade Date	ER Date	Ex Div Date	Entry Trade Expiry Date	Entry Stock Price [$/sh]	Entry Put Strike Price [$]	Entry Put Option Price [$/sh]	# Shares
NVDA	Computer	8/20/21	11/18/21	12/17/21	09/24/21	$ 208.16	$ 200.00	$ 5.65	100

Figure 82: NVDA: Entering Our Initial Trade

Initial trade returns

CASH SECURED PUT TRADE ENTRY							
OPENING TRADE							
Expected # Of Days In Trade [#]	Time Value [$/sh]	Put Premium Collected Per Contract [$]	Cash Req/Cont [$]	Breakeven [$/sh]	Return On Option ROO [%]	Return On Option ROO Annual'zd [%]	ROO Premium [$]
36	$ 5.65	$ 565.00	$ 19,435.00	$ 194.35	2.91%	29.48%	$ 565.00

Purchase Discount If Exercised [%]	Stock Cost/Share If Exercised [$/sh]	Total Capital Invested [$]
6.63%	$ 194.35	$ 19,435.00

Figure 83: NVDA: Initial Trade Returns

The Trade Management Calculator shows an initial return on the option of 2.91%, 29.48% annualized based on a 36-day trade. If the put is exercised, shares will be purchased at a 6.63% discount at the breakeven price point of $194.35.

How to manage closing ITM strikes and exiting the trade

The original put trade is closed by entering the current price of the stock on expiration Friday and the BTC cost to close the ITM short put.

Trade adjustment entries

CASH SECURED PUT TRADE MANAGEMENT								
				CLOSING TRADE				
Stock Symbol	Exit Strategy Selected	Adjust. Trade Date	Adjust. Expiry Date	BTC Entry Option Price [$/Sh]	STO Entry #2 Strike Price [$/Sh]	STO Entry #2 Option Premium [$/Sh]	Current Stock Price Basis [$]	Price of Stock At Time of Exercise [$]
NVDA	Close ITM Strike & Exit	09/24/21		$ 1.10			$ 199.00	

Figure 84: NVDA: Closing ITM Strike Adjustments

Final calculations after closing and ITM strike and exiting

Final Net Option Profit/Loss [$/Sh]	Final Net Option Profit/Loss [$]	Final Net Option Return [%]	Unrealized Final Stock Profit/Loss [$]	Unrealized Final Stock $ Total Stock Profit/Loss [$]	Unreal. Final Stock % Total Stock Profit/Loss [%]	Combined Final Trade Total Profit/Loss [$]	Combined Final Trade Total Profit/Loss [%]
$ 4.55	$ 455.00	2.34%	$ -	$ -	0.00%	$ 455.00	2.34%

Figure 85: NVDA: Final Results After Closing the ITM Put

The spreadsheet will reflect the initial time-value return minus the cost-to-close debit. In this case, the net option profit is $455.00 ($565.00 - $110.00), resulting in a 36-day return of 2.34%. The initial time-value return was 2.91%. This process allows us to exit a trade that does not align with our system requirements and goals.

Discussion

Closing and exiting an ITM put trade can be considered as expiration approaches when the underlying security no longer meets our system requirements. The final results will be lower than the initial time-value returns because of the cost-to-close debit. It may even result in a loss, if the cost-to-close is greater than the initial premium credit. However, in most of these net debit scenarios, we would have mitigated earlier with exit strategy implementation. Not every trade will have successful results but mitigating losses is as important as enhancing gains. Closing ITM strikes can result in a net credit or debit.

Chapter 21

Expire Worthless (Take no action on OTM Puts)

What is allowing an OTM put strike to expire worthless?

In the BCI methodology, we favor out-of-the-money (OTM) put strikes (lower than current market value at the time of the trade). This will generate an initial time-value return as well as placing us in a position to purchase the underlying security at a discount, if exercised. If the option strike price remains OTM through expiration, no action is needed as the option expires worthless and we realize that initial time-value return.

When to consider allowing an ITM strike to expire worthless?

We use this strategy approach when the stock price remains above the put strike through expiration. On the Monday, after expiration Friday, the cash used to secure the original put trade is now freed up to secure another put sale in the next contract cycle. We will continue to use our NVDA example to highlight this strategy approach.

Real-life example with NVIDIA Corp. (Nasdaq: NVDA)

- 8/20/2021: NVDA trading at $208.16
- 8/20/2021: STO the 9/24/2021 $200.00 put at $5.65

- 9/24/2021, NVDA is trading at $205.00, resulting in the original short put strike ($200.00) to expire out-the-money.

Initial trade entries

Stock Symbol	Industry	Entry Trade Date	ER Date	Ex Div Date	Entry Trade Expiry Date	Entry Stock Price [$/sh]	Entry Put Strike Price [$]	Entry Put Option Price [$/sh]	# Shares
NVDA	Computer	8/20/21	11/18/21	12/17/21	09/24/21	$ 208.16	$ 200.00	$ 5.65	100

Figure 86: NVDA: Entering Our Initial Trade

Initial trade returns

CASH SECURED PUT TRADE ENTRY							
OPENING TRADE							
Expected # Of Days In Trade [#]	Time Value [$/sh]	Put Premium Collected Per Contract [$]	Cash Req/Cont [$]	Breakeven [$/sh]	Return On Option ROO [%]	Return On Option ROO Annual'zd [%]	ROO Premium [$]
36	$ 5.65	$ 565.00	$ 19,435.00	$ 194.35	2.91%	29.48%	$ 565.00

Purchase Discount If Exercised [%]	Stock Cost/Share If Exercised [$/sh]	Total Capital Invested [$]
6.63%	$ 194.35	$ 19,435.00

Figure 87: NVDA: Initial Trade Returns

The Trade Management Calculator shows an initial return on the option of 2.91%, 29.48% annualized based on a 36-day trade. If exercised, shares are purchased at a cost-basis of

$194.35, a discount of 6.63% from the original price of NVDA when the put trade was first executed.

How to manage allowing our options to expire worthless

We enter the contract expiration date and the price of the security at expiration.

Trade adjustment entries

						CLOSING TRADE		
Stock Symbol	Exit Strategy Selected	Adjust. Trade Date	Adjust. Expiry Date	BTC Entry Option Price [$/Sh]	STO Entry #2 Strike Price [$/Sh]	STO Entry #2 Option Premium [$/Sh]	Current Stock Price Basis [$]	Price of Stock At Time of Exercise [$]
NVDA	Expire Worthless	09/24/21					$ 205.00	

Figure 88: NVDA: Allowing to Expire Worthless Adjustments

Final results after allowing to expire worthless

Final Net Option Profit/Loss [$/Sh]	Final Net Option Profit/Loss [$]	Final Net Option Return [%]	Unrealized Final Stock Profit/Loss [$]	Unrealized Final Stock $ Total Stock Profit/Loss [$]	Unreal. Final Stock % Total Stock Profit/Loss [%]	Combined Final Trade Total Profit/Loss [$]	Combined Final Trade Total Profit/Loss [%]
$ 5.65	$ 565.00	2.91%	$ -	$ -	0.00%	$ 565.00	2.91%

Figure 89: NVDA: Final Results After Allowing to Expire Worthless

The spreadsheet a final time-value option return of $5.65 per-share or 2.91% (green cells). The final combined trade profit (no share credit or debit) is $565.00 or 2.91% (yellow cells). This is the same percentage return as the initial return when the trade was originally executed.

The cash set aside to secure this expiring put ($19,435.00) is now freed up to secure another put after expiration Friday.

Discussion

We consider allowing an OTM put strike to expire worthless when the share value remains above the put strike through contract expiration. The initial time-value return is realized. The cash freed up to secure another put the Monday or Tuesday after expiration Friday can be to secure another put with the same or different underlying security.

Chapter 22

Rolling-Down an ITM Strike

What is rolling-down an ITM put strike?

When share price moves down below the (once OTM) put strike, the strike is now in-the-money (ITM). This creates a scenario where exercise is more likely. Rolling-down our put strike involves buying back the short put and selling another at lower strike price with the same expiration date. Since there is a greater intrinsic-value component to the higher strike put, the trade will generally result in a net cash debit.

When to consider rolling-down an ITM strike?

We use this strategy approach when the stock price moves below the put strike prior to expiration. If we do not want the shares *put* to us, we must close the short put. To mitigate this cost-to-close, we can sell a lower strike (generally out-of-the-money) which will partially mitigate the closing debit.

Real-life example with NetApp, Inc. (Nasdaq: NTAP)

- 12/18/2017: With NTAP trading at $58.50
- 12/18/2017: STO the slightly out-of-the-money $58.00 put for $2.00
- 1/2/2018: Share price declines to $55.32
- 1/2/2018: Consider rolling-down to the OTM $54.00 put strike

Initial trade entries

Stock Symbol	Industry	Entry Trade Date	ER Date	Ex Div Date	Entry Trade Expiry Date	Entry Stock Price [$/sh]	Entry Put Strike Price [$]	Entry Put Option Price [$/sh]	# Shares
NTAP	Software	12/18/17	11/25/17	10/07/17	01/19/18	$ 58.50	$ 58.00	$ 2.00	100

Figure 90: NTAP: Entering Our Initial Trade

Initial trade returns

OPENING TRADE							
Expected # Of Days In Trade [#]	Time Value [$/sh]	Put Premium Collected Per Contract [$]	Cash Req/Cont [$]	Breakeven [$/sh]	Return On Option ROO [%]	Return On Option ROO Annual'zd [%]	ROO Premium [$]
33	$ 2.00	$ 200.00	$ 5,600.00	$ 56.00	3.57%	39.50%	$ 200.00

Purchase Discount If Exercised [%]	Stock Cost/Share If Exercised [$/sh]	Total Capital Invested [$]
4.27%	$ 56.00	$ 5,600.00

Figure 91: NTAP: Initial Put Trade Returns

The Trade Management Calculator shows an initial return on the option of 3.57%, 39.50% annualized, based on a 33-day trade (brown cells). If the put is allowed to be exercised, shares will be purchased at a 4.27% discount from the original market price (green cell). The breakeven price point is $56.00 (yellow cell).

Rolling-down option-chain on 1/2/2018 (from the $58.00 to the $54.00 put strike)

NTAP Put Option Chain on 1/2/2018

		Strike		Bid	Ask
	2017-12-27 12:56PM EST	53.50	0.38	0.40	0.46
	2017-12-29 11:09AM EST	54.00	0.50	0.52	0.58
	2017-12-29 11:51PM EST	54.50	0.60	0.67	0.78
NTAP180119P00055000	2017-12-29 3:45PM EST	55.00	0.89	0.88	0.96
NTAP180119P00055500	2017-12-29 12:51PM EST	55.50	1.08	1.12	1.23
NTAP180119P00056000	2017-12-22 11:47PM EST	56.00	0.72	0.98	1.15
NTAP180119P00056500	2017-12-27 11:42AM EST	56.50	1.49	1.72	1.89
NTAP180119P00057000	2017-12-27 1:05PM EST	57.00	1.89	2.02	2.22
NTAP180119P00057500	2017-12-22 11:47PM EST	57.50	1.22	1.83	2.04
NTAP180119P00058000	2017-12-29 11:51PM EST	58.00	2.74	2.93	3.10
NTAP180119P00060000	2017-12-26 11:18AM EST	60.00	4.34	4.60	5.10

Figure 92: NTAP: Put Option-Chain on 1/2/2018

How to manage our rolling-down trades

We enter the BTC price for the original $58.00 strike and the STO premium on the new, lower OTM $54.00 strike. We also enter the current market value of the underlying security, $55.32, in this example, as well as the trade adjustment date.

Trade adjustment entries

CASH SECURED PUT TRADE MANAGEMENT								
				CLOSING TRADE				
Stock Symbol	Exit Strategy Selected	Adjust. Trade Date	Adjust. Expiry Date	BTC Entry Option Price [$/Sh]	STO Entry #2 Strike Price [$/Sh]	STO Entry #2 Option Premium [$/Sh]	Current Stock Price Basis [$]	Price of Stock At Time of Exercise [$]
NTAP	Roll-Down	01/02/18	01/19/18	$ 3.10	$ 54.00	$ 0.52	$ 55.32	

Figure 93: NTAP: Rolling-Down Trade Adjustments

The $58.00 strike is rolled-down to the $54.00 strike (green cell) at a net debit of $2.58 ($3.10 -$0.52).

Final calculations after the rolling-down trade adjustment

						FINAL RESULT	
Final Net Option Profit/Loss [$/Sh]	Final Net Option Profit/Loss [$]	Final Net Option Return [%]	Unrealized Final Stock Profit/Loss [$]	Unrealized Final Stock $ Total Stock Profit/Loss [$]	Unreal. Final Stock % Total Stock Profit/Loss [%]	Combined Final Trade Total Profit/Loss [$]	Combined Final Trade Total Profit/Loss [%]
$ (0.58)	$ (58.00)	-1.04%	$ -	$ -	0.00%	$ (58.00)	-1.04%

Figure 94: NTAP: Final Results After Rolling-Down

The post-adjusted time-value option return calculates to -$0.58 per-share, $58.00 per-contract (yellow cells) or -1.04% (green cell). Exercise will be avoided as long as share value remains above the new OTM $54.00 strike ($55.32 at the time of the roll-down).

Do we roll-down routinely to mitigate losses when trades turn against us?

No. Although rolling down should definitely be in our exit strategy arsenal, there needs to be a thought process before making a decision to execute such a trade. With covered call writing, we own the underlying, so, to close a position in its entirety we would need to both buy back the option and sell the underlying.

With put-selling, once we buy back the short put, we have no contractual obligation and do not own the underlying. Selling another option while early to mid-contract is a no-brainer, but using the same underlying is not. It is instructive to remember that the stock in question has already under-performed our expectations. Do we want to stay committed to this, now, under-performer? The guideline I use is a comparison of the recent performance of the stock compared to that of the S&P 500. Let's have a look at a comparison chart of NTAP compared to the S&P 500 over the time frame of the trade to date:

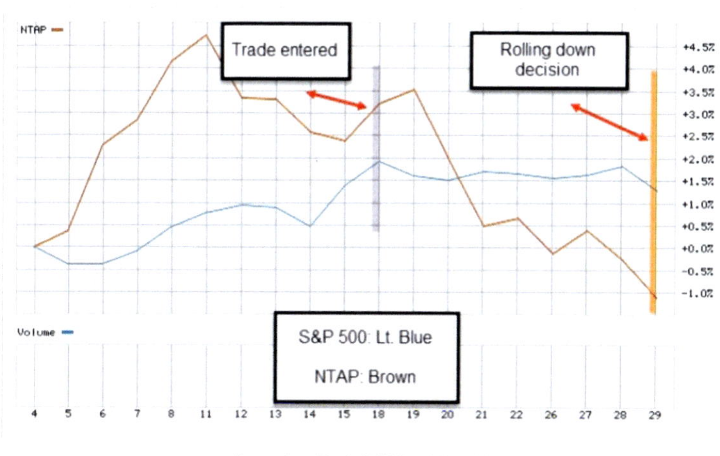

Figure 95: Comparison Chart of NTAP versus the S&P 500

Note the following:

- When the trade was entered (purple bar), NTAP (brown line) was trading above the S&P 500
- On December 20th, there was a bearish movement of NTAP price movement to below that of the S&P 500
- On 1/2/2018 (gold bar), NTAP price continued to decline and remained under the price action of the S&P 500
- Had the price movement of NTAP remained above that of the S&P 500, I would strongly consider rolling-down
- In a case like this one, I would reject rolling-down and enter a new put sale with a different underlying to mitigate the current loss of $1.10 per share ($3.10 – $2.00)

What about rolling-out-and-down?

I prefer not to extend my trades on under-performing securities to a later date. We screened these stocks and ETFs from fundamental, technical and common-sense perspectives and yet the price dropped below the breakeven price point. Where is the cash used to secure our puts best placed …in this under-performer of in a new, better-performing underlying? *I, generally, reserve rolling-down in-the-money puts to the same contract cycle.*

Discussion

Rolling down a short put is part of our position management arsenal but should be mainly implemented in scenarios when declining share price leaves the initial put strike ITM while still out-performing the overall market.

Chapter 23

Rolling-In

Over the years, we have discussed rolling options as an integral part of our position management arsenal. This chapter will detail a new rolling strategy developed by BCI … rolling-in.

What is rolling-in as it relates to the other rolling strategies?

- *Rolling-up:* Close out options at a lower strike and open options at a higher strike
- *Rolling-down:* Closing out options at one strike price and opening options at a lower strike price
- *Rolling-out (forward):* Closing out options at a near-term expiration and opening at the same strike at a later date
- *Rolling-in:* Closing out options at a current-term expiration and opening at the same strike at an earlier date

When to consider rolling-in

Avoid risky corporate or market events

- Earnings reports
- Fed announcement
- FDA product announcement
- Corporate news conference
- Political events

Personal business commitments: unavailable to monitor trades

- Family vacation
- Business trip
- Hospital stays/medical reasons

Must liquidate position by a specific date

- Cash needed for other obligations

Real-life example with Energy Select Sector SPDR Fund (NYSE: XLE):

- 2/28/2022: XLE trading at $68.09
- 2/28/2022: STO 1 x 3/18/2022 $66.00 put at $1.40
- 3/7/2022: XLE trading at $75.23
- 3/7/2022: BTC the 3/18/2022 $66.00 put at $0.25
- 3/7/2022: STO the 3/11/2022 $66.00 put at $0.08 (roll-in from 3/18/2022 to 3/11/2022)

Initial trade entries

Stock Symbol	Industry	Entry Trade Date	ER Date	Ex Div Date	Entry Trade Expiry Date	Entry Stock Price [$/sh]	Entry Put Strike Price [$]	Entry Put Option Price [$/sh]	# Shares
XLE	Energy	2/28/22	NA	03/20/22	03/18/22	$ 68.09	$ 66.00	$ 1.40	100

Figure 96: XLE: Entering Out Initial Trade

Initial trade returns

OPENING TRADE							
Expected # Of Days In Trade [#]	Time Value [$/sh]	Put Premium Collected Per Contract [$]	Cash Req/Cont [$]	Breakeven [$/sh]	Return On Option ROO [%]	Return On Option ROO Annual'zd [%]	ROO Premium [$]
19	$ 1.40	$ 140.00	$ 6,460.00	$ 64.60	2.17%	41.63%	$ 140.00

Purchase Discount If Exercised [%]	Stock Cost/Share If Exercised [$/sh]	Total Capital Invested [$]
5.13%	$ 64.60	$ 6,460.00

Figure 97: XLE: Initial Trade Returns

The spreadsheet shows an initial time-value return of 2.17%, 41.63% annualized based on a 19-day trade. The purchase discount percent, if exercised, is 5.13%.

How to manage rolling-in

Enter the date of the adjustment and the new, shorter-term expiration date along with the BTC and STO premiums. The strike remains the same and the current share price is noted.

Trade adjustment entries

CASH SECURED PUT TRADE MANAGEMENT								
						CLOSING TRADE		
Stock Symbol	Exit Strategy Selected	Adjust. Trade Date	Adjust. Expiry Date	BTC Entry Option Price [$/Sh]	STO Entry #2 Strike Price [$/Sh]	STO Entry #2 Option Premium [$/Sh]	Current Stock Price Basis [$]	Price of Stock At Time of Exercise [$]
XLE	Roll-In	03/07/22	03/11/22	$ 0.25	$ 66.00	$ 0.08	$ 75.23	

Figure 98: XLE: Rolling-In Trade Adjustments

The 3/18/2022 expiration was rolled-in to the 3/11/2022 expiration at a net option debit of $0.17 ($0.25 - $0.08).

Final calculations

Final Net Option Profit/Loss [$/Sh]	Final Net Option Profit/Loss [$]	Final Net Option Return [%]	Unrealized Final Stock Profit/Loss [$]	Unrealized Final Stock $ Total Stock Profit/Loss [$]	Unreal. Final Stock % Total Stock Profit/Loss [%]
$ 1.23	$ 123.00	1.90%	$ -	$ -	0.00%

FINAL RESULT	
Combined Final Trade Total Profit/Loss [$]	Combined Final Trade Total Profit/Loss [%]
$ 123.00	1.90%

Figure 99: XLE: Final Results After Rolling-In

The final rolled-in 25-day return is now 1.90%, a slight decrease from the original 2.17%, but a risky event was avoided. The slight decrease in the return on the option can be mitigated and possibly turned into a net gain by re-investing the cash during the remaining time of that monthly contract using a different security.

Discussion

Rolling-in is a new and additional position management technique that can be utilized to avoid risky events as well as allow for better management and needs. The cost to roll-in will typically be low or even result in a higher annualized return but will lower the overall risk of our portfolio positions.

Chapter 24
Rolling-Out ITM Strikes

What is rolling-out an ITM put strike?

This is where we buy back (buy-to-close or BTC) the short put as expiration approaches and immediately sell the same strike put option in the next contract cycle.

When to consider rolling-out an ITM strike

If a strike is in-the-money as expiration approaches, we may opt to roll the trade rather than close and exit the current option position. Reasons to take this approach include:

- We do not want to take possession of the shares (*put* to us)
- There is no upcoming earnings report in the next contract cycle
- The underlying security still meets our system requirements (fundamental, technical and common-sense screens)
- The rolling calculations do meet our stated initial time-value return goal range

Difference between rolling and exiting an ITM put strike as expiration approaches

When we roll the option, we BTC the near-term strike and STO the next contract same put strike. If we decide to close the ITM strike and simply exit the trade, we only close the current put trade and look to establish a new cash-secured put trade with a different security at the start of the next contract cycle. We will use a real-example with NVDA to demonstrate a rolling-out example.

Real-life example with NVIDIA Corp. (Nasdaq: NVDA)

- 8/20/2021: NVDA trading at $208.16
- 8/20/2021: STO 1 x 9/24/2021 $200.00 put at $5.65
- 9/24/2021: On expiration Friday, NVDA is trading at $199.00, leaving the original short put strike ($200.00) in-the-money.
- 9/24/2021: BTC cost is $1.10
- 9/24/2021: STO the next month $200.00 put at $5.00
- 9/24/2021: A decision is made to roll rather than close the trade

Initial trade entries

Stock Symbol	Industry	Entry Trade Date	ER Date	Ex Div Date	Entry Trade Expiry Date	Entry Stock Price [$/sh]	Entry Put Strike Price [$]	Entry Put Option Price [$/sh]	# Shares
NVDA	Semi Cond.	8/20/21	11/18/21	09/27/21	09/24/21	$ 208.16	$ 200.00	$ 5.65	100

Figure 100: NVDA: Entering Our Initial Trade

Initial trade returns

OPENING TRADE							
Expected # Of Days In Trade [#]	Time Value [$/sh]	Put Premium Collected Per Contract [$]	Cash Req/Cont [$]	Breakeven [$/sh]	Return On Option ROO [%]	Return On Option ROO Annual'zd [%]	ROO Premium [$]
36	$ 5.65	$ 565.00	$ 19,435.00	$ 194.35	2.91%	29.48%	$ 565.00

Purchase Discount If Exercised [%]	Stock Cost/Share If Exercised [$/sh]	Total Capital Invested [$]
6.63%	$ 194.35	$ 19,435.00

Figure 101: NVDA: Initial Put Trade Returns

The Trade Management Calculator shows an initial return on the option of 2.91%, 29.48% annualized based on a 36-day trade. If the put is exercised, NVDA is purchased at a cost-basis of $194.35, a 6.63% discount from the stock price when the put sale was executed.

How to manage our rolling-out to ITM strike trades

Our current contract month trade is completed as initially structured. The final time-value return is the same as the initial time-value return. The current value of the underlying security is entered into our spreadsheet (trading log) as well as the contract expiration date. The rolling-out trade is then continued in the next contract cycle where the current market value (ending value at expiration of the expiring contract) is entered, and the net option credit is also entered with the next expiration date. The net option credit consists of the new premium less the cost-to-close debit from the previous contract. This is shown in the upcoming screenshots.

Trade adjustment entries

Stock Symbol	Exit Strategy Selected	Adjust. Trade Date	Adjust. Expiry Date	BTC Entry Option Price [$/Sh]	STO Entry #2 Strike Price [$/Sh]	STO Entry #2 Option Premium [$/Sh]	Current Stock Price Basis [$]	Price of Stock At Time of Exercise [$]
NVDA	Roll-Out	09/24/21					$ 199.00	

Figure 102: NVDA: Rolling-Out Trade Adjustments

Final calculations prior to rolling the ITM strike

Final Net Option Profit/Loss [$/Sh]	Final Net Option Profit/Loss [$]	Final Net Option Return [%]	Unrealized Final Stock Profit/Loss [$]	Unrealized Final Stock $ Total Stock Profit/Loss [$]	Unreal. Final Stock % Total Stock Profit/Loss [%]
$ 5.65	$ 565.00	2.91%	$ -	$ -	0.00%

FINAL RESULT	
Combined Final Trade Total Profit/Loss [$]	Combined Final Trade Total Profit/Loss [%]
$ 565.00	2.91%

Figure 103: NVDA: Final Results Prior to Rolling the Option

The spreadsheet will reflect the final time-value return to be the same as the initial time-value return (2.91%) as well as the same total net income of $565.00 per-contract.

Initial entries for the rolled-out trade in the next contract cycle

Stock Symbol	Industry	Entry Trade Date	ER Date	Ex Div Date	Entry Trade Expiry Date	Entry Stock Price [$/sh]	Entry Put Strike Price [$]	Entry Put Option Price [$/sh]	# Shares
NVDA	Semi Cond.	9/24/21	11/18/21	09/27/21	10/15/21	$ 199.00	$ 200.00	$ 3.90	100

Figure 104: NVDA: Entering the Rolled-Out Trade into the Next Contract Cycle

The price of NVDA at the time of the roll was $199.00 and the net BTC and STO premium for the $200.00 strike was $3.90 ($5.00 - $1.10).

Initial trade returns for the rolled-out put

OPENING TRADE							
Expected # Of Days In Trade [#]	Time Value [$/sh]	Put Premium Collected Per Contract [$]	Cash Req/Cont [$]	Breakeven [$/sh]	Return On Option ROO [%]	Return On Option ROO Annual'zd [%]	ROO Premium [$]
22	$ 3.90	$ 390.00	$ 19,610.00	$ 196.10	1.99%	33.00%	$ 390.00

Purchase Discount If Exercised [%]	Stock Cost/Share If Exercised [$/sh]	Total Capital Invested [$]
1.46%	$ 196.10	$ 19,610.00

Figure 105: NVDA: Initial Next Contract Trade Returns After Rolling-Out

The calculator displays a 22-day return of 1.99% (brown cell), 33.00% annualized (green cell) based on a 22-day trade. The breakeven price point is $196.10 (yellow cell) and, if exercised, shares are purchased at a discount of 1.46% (pink cell).

Discussion

We consider rolling-out an ITM put strike when the security still meets all system criteria, and the calculations align with our stated initial time-value return goal range. The initial trade is closed reflecting the initial time-value return and the current security price and net option credit is entered into the next contract cycle.

Chapter 25

Rolling-Up Deep OTM Put Strikes

What is rolling-up deep OTM put strikes?

When share price moves up significantly, the put strike is now much deeper out-of-the-money (OTM). Since share value and put value are inversely related (this explains the negative sign (-) associated with put Deltas), put values will decline. This creates an exit strategy opportunity to buy back the short put at a much lower price than the original put sale. Once the short put is closed, another put can be sold at a higher strike which is still out-of-the-money and will result in a net option credit. In essence, we have created a second income stream in the same contract month.

When to consider rolling-up an OTM strike

We use this strategy approach when the stock price moves significantly higher and we can sell another higher OTM put strike that will generate a net option credit while still meeting our system requirements. This exit strategy is frequently used in conjunction with our 10-Delta put strategy, where all strikes are sold with Deltas of 10 or less resulting in approximately a 90+% probability of avoiding exercise.

Real-life example with InMode Ltd. (Nasdaq: INMD)

- 9/20/2021: INMD treading at $136.00
- 9/20/2021: STO 1 x 10/15/2021 $110.00 put at $0.95

- 9/21/2021: BTC 1 x 10/15/2021 $110.00 put at 0.58
- 9/21/2021: STO 1 x 10/15/2021 $120.00 put at $1.05
- 9/21/2021: INMD trading at $144.00

Initial trade entries

Stock Symbol	Industry	Entry Trade Date	ER Date	Ex Div Date	Entry Trade Expiry Date	Entry Stock Price [$/sh]	Entry Put Strike Price [$]	Entry Put Option Price [$/sh]	# Shares
INMD	Medical	9/20/21	11/12/21	NA	10/15/21	$ 136.00	$ 110.00	$ 0.95	100

Figure 106: INMD: Entering Our Initial Trade

Initial trade returns

OPENING TRADE							
Expected # Of Days In Trade [#]	Time Value [$/sh]	Put Premium Collected Per Contract [$]	Cash Req/Cont [$]	Breakeven [$/sh]	Return On Option ROO [%]	Return On Option ROO Annual'zd [%]	ROO Premium [$]
26	$ 0.95	$ 95.00	$ 10,905.00	$ 109.05	0.87%	12.23%	$ 95.00

Purchase Discount If Exercised [%]	Stock Cost/Share If Exercised [$/sh]	Total Capital Invested [$]
19.82%	$ 109.05	$ 10,905.00

Figure 107: INMD: Initial Put Trade Returns

The Trade Management Calculator shows an initial return on the option of 0.87%, 12.23% annualized (brown cells), based on a 26-day trade. If the put is allowed to be exercised, shares will be purchased at a 19.82% discount from the original market price (green cell). The breakeven price point is $109.05(yellow cell).

How to manage rolling-up trades

The trade adjustment date is entered along with the BTC and STO premiums. We enter the new higher strike price and the price of the stock at the time of the roll.

Trade adjustment entries

CASH SECURED PUT TRADE MANAGEMENT								
						CLOSING TRADE		
Stock Symbol	Exit Strategy Selected	Adjust. Trade Date	Adjust. Expiry Date	BTC Entry Option Price [$/Sh]	STO Entry #2 Strike Price [$/Sh]	STO Entry #2 Option Premium [$/Sh]	Current Stock Price Basis [$]	Price of Stock At Time of Exercise [$]
INMD	Roll-Up	09/21/21		$ 0.58	$ 120.00	$ 1.05	$ 144.00	

Figure 108: INMD: Rolling-Up Trade Adjustments

The $110.00 strike is rolled-up to the $120.00 strike (green cell) at a net credit of $0.47 ($1.05 -$0.58) with the current share value at $144.00.

Final calculations through the rolling-up trade adjustment

Final Net Option Profit/Loss [$/Sh]	Final Net Option Profit/Loss [$]	Final Net Option Return [%]	Unrealized Final Stock Profit/Loss [$]	Unrealized Final Stock $ Total Stock Profit/Loss [$]	Unreal. Final Stock % Total Stock Profit/Loss [%]
$ 1.42	$ 142.00	1.30%	$ -	$ -	0.00%

FINAL RESULT	
Combined Final Trade Total Profit/Loss [$]	Combined Final Trade Total Profit/Loss [%]
$ 142.00	1.30%

Figure 109: INMD: Final Results After Rolling-Up

The spreadsheet will calculate the post-adjusted time-value option return of $1.42 per-share, $142.00 per-contract (yellow cells) or 1.30% (green cell). This is an increase from the initial time-value return of 0.87%. Exercise will be avoided as long as share value remains above the new OTM $120.00 strike ($144.00 at the time of the roll).

Discussion

Rolling-up a short put is part of our position management arsenal and should be considered when share value rises substantially after initial trade execution. The trade should result in a net option credit while still adhering to system guidelines regarding the safety of our trades (new strikes should still be OTM especially if avoiding exercise is a strategy goal). This strategy can be used multiple times in a given month under the right conditions such as an increasing share price over the monthly option cycle.

Chapter 26

Using Multiple Exit Strategies in the Same Contract Cycle

What is using multiple exit strategies in the same contract cycle?

There are situations where multiple exit strategy opportunities present in the same contract month. In this Nvidia (Nasdaq: NVDA) example, we will use the *20% guideline* to close the original trade and *setup a 2nd put sale in the same contract cycle*. These trades represent 2 income streams in the same contract cycle. A hypothetical second trade will be used to demonstrate this approach.

When to consider using multiple exit strategies

After we have executed one exit strategy opportunity, we are always alert for additional adjustment situations.

What is the 20% guideline?

This guideline gives us a parameter that assists us in determining when to close our short put position should share value accelerate significantly in the first 2 weeks of a 4-week contract or the first 3 weeks of a 5-week contract. When share value rises substantially causing put value to decline, we should consider closing the short put position retaining 80% of the original premium profit and moving to a new cash-secured put trade with a different underlying security.

This action will create an opportunity to generate an additional income stream in the same contract cycle with a similar cash investment. See Chapter 18 for more information on the 20% guideline.

Real-life example with Nvidia Corp. (Nasdaq: NVDA)

- 8/20/2021: NVDA trading at $208.16
- 8/20/2021: STO 1 x 9/24/2021 $200.00 put at $5.65
- 9/2/2021: NVDA trading at $215.50
- 9/2/2021: The cost-to-close the $200.00 strike is $1.10, meeting the 20% guideline threshold ($1.13 is 20% of $5.65)
- 9/2/2021: After closing the trade, we now can set up a new trade, a second income stream, *in the same contract month*, with a new underlying security

Initial trade entries

Stock Symbol	Industry	Entry Trade Date	ER Date	Ex Div Date	Entry Trade Expiry Date	Entry Stock Price [$/sh]	Entry Put Strike Price [$]	Entry Put Option Price [$/sh]	# Shares
NVDA	Computer	8/20/21	11/18/21	12/17/21	09/24/21	$ 208.16	$ 200.00	$ 5.65	100

Figure 110: NVDA: Entering Our Initial Put Trade

Initial trade calculations and the 20% guideline

OPENING TRADE							
Expected # Of Days In Trade [#]	Time Value [$/sh]	Put Premium Collected Per Contract [$]	Cash Req/Cont [$]	Breakeven [$/sh]	Return On Option ROO [%]	Return On Option ROO Annual'zd [%]	ROO Premium [$]
36	$ 5.65	$ 565.00	$ 19,435.00	$ 194.35	2.91%	29.48%	$ 565.00

Purchase Discount If Exercised [%]	Stock Cost/Share If Exercised [$/sh]	Total Capital Invested [$]	3% Stock Exit Guideline [$]	20% Optn Exit Guideline [$]	10% Optn Exit Guideline [$]
6.63%	$ 194.35	$ 19,435.00	$ 194.00	$ 1.13	$ 0.57

Figure 111: NVDA: Initial Trade Returns and the 20% BTC Price Point Guideline

The initial return on the option (ROO) is 2.91%, 29.48% annualized based on a 36-day trade. If the put option is exercised, the purchase discount is 6.63%. The 20% guideline sets a threshold price to buy-to-close the short put at $1.13 or lower. Note that $19,435.00 per-contract was required to secure the put trade.

Practical application

After entering the initial trade, set a buy-to-close (BTC) limit order good-until-cancelled (GTC) at $1.13. If the platform only accepts these orders in $0.05 increments, set the BTC GTC limit order at $1.15.

Trade adjustment entries

						CLOSING TRADE		
Stock Symbol	Exit Strategy Selected	Adjust. Trade Date	Adjust. Expiry Date	BTC Entry Option Price [$/Sh]	STO Entry #2 Strike Price [$/Sh]	STO Entry #2 Option Premium [$/Sh]	Current Stock Price Basis [$]	Price of Stock At Time of Exercise [$]
NVDA	20% Option Buy-Back Gdln	09/02/21		$ 1.10			$ 215.50	

Figure 112: NVDA: 20% Guideline Trade Adjustments

The trade date, BTC premium and the current value of the shares are entered.

Initial trade final calculations

Final Net Option Profit/Loss [$/Sh]	Final Net Option Profit/Loss [$]	Final Net Option Return [%]	Unrealized Final Stock Profit/Loss [$]	Unrealized Final Stock $ Total Stock Profit/Loss [$]	Unreal. Final Stock % Total Stock Profit/Loss [%]
$ 4.55	$ 455.00	2.34%	$ -	$ -	0.00%

FINAL RESULT	
Combined Final Trade Total Profit/Loss [$]	Combined Final Trade Total Profit/Loss [%]
$ 455.00	2.34%

Figure 113: NVDA: Final Results After Implementing the 20% Guideline

The Trade Management Calculator shows a realized return of $455.00 per-contract which represents a 2.34%, 13-day realized return (8/20/21 – 9/2/2021).

The original $19,435.00 is now freed up to secure another put trade in the same contract month with a new security. Using a different underlying will protect us from potential profit-taking of this recently robustly appreciated stock.

Entering the 2nd trade in the same contract month (second income stream)

We will use a hypothetical stock, BCI, and using the freed up $19,435.00 cash to secure this new put trade (row highlighted in green).

Stock Symbol	Industry	Entry Trade Date	ER Date	Ex Div Date	Entry Trade Expiry Date	Entry Stock Price [$/sh]	Entry Put Strike Price [$]	Entry Put Option Price [$/sh]	# Shares
NVDA	Computer	8/20/21	11/18/21	12/17/21	09/24/21	$ 208.16	$ 200.00	$ 5.65	100
ABC		12/27/21			01/21/22	$ 51.00	$ 50.00	$ 1.50	200
DEF		12/27/21			01/21/22	$ 51.00	$ 50.00	$ 1.50	100
GHI		12/27/21			01/21/22	$ 51.00	$ 50.00	$ 1.50	300
JKL		12/27/21			01/21/22	$ 51.00	$ 50.00	$ 1.50	100
MNO		12/27/21			01/21/22	$ 51.00	$ 50.00	$ 1.50	400
PQR		12/27/21			01/21/22	$ 51.00	$ 50.00	$ 1.50	100
STV		12/27/21			01/21/22	$ 51.00	$ 50.00	$ 1.50	300
WXY		12/27/21			01/21/22	$ 51.00	$ 50.00	$ 1.50	100
ZAB		12/27/21			01/21/22	$ 51.00	$ 50.00	$ 1.50	400
BCI		09/02/21			09/24/21	$ 51.00	$ 50.00	$ 1.50	400

Figure 114: BCI: Initial Post-20% Guideline Entries

The brown-highlighted row shows the initial trade entries for the first trade and the green-highlighted row reflects the second trade which leverages the *same cash investment* as the NVDA trade. Note we sold 4 contracts because BCI share price was approximately 1/4th that of NVDA.

Total capital invested hypothetical after second trade entry

Return On Option ROO [%]	Return On Option ROO Annual'zd [%]	ROO Premium [$]	Purchase Discount If Exercised [%]	Stock Cost/Share If Exercised [$/sh]	Total Capital Invested [$]
3.09%	49.08%	$ 600.00	4.90%	$ 48.50	$ 19,400.00

Figure 115: BCI: Initial Second-Trade Returns Showing Duplicated Capital Investment

The spreadsheet shows an additional capital investment for this second trade in the same contract cycle of $19,400.00, when, in reality, it is the same cash investment freed up from the initial put sale. This is misleading because the same cash investment is used in the second trade and will skew the *final total % portfolio returns.*

How to correct total cash invested after entering a second trade in the same contract cycle

We scroll down and enter a *capital adjustment* of -$19,400.00 into the *capital adjustment section* of the spreadsheet. Enter a negative total capital invested at the bottom of Column V (blue cell under Column V) and the corresponding ticker symbol is noted in column A (blue cell). The proper Total Capital Invested will now be calculated for our total portfolio capital invested (red arrow). Figures 116 and 117 show overview and close-up views of the capital adjustment section of the spreadsheet.

Capital adjustment entry section overview

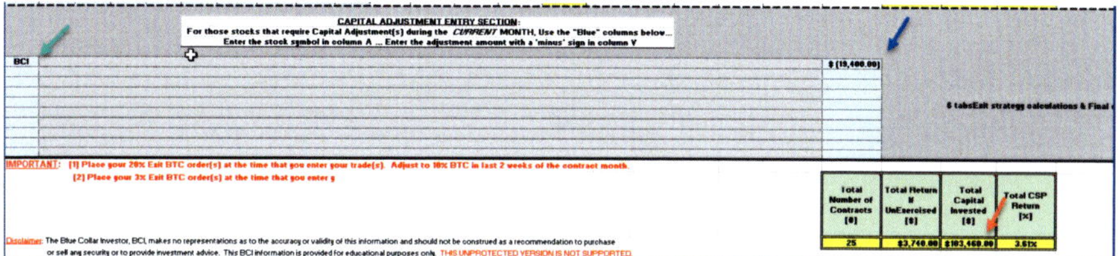

Figure 116: Capital Adjustment Entry Section

Capital adjustment entry section: Close-up views

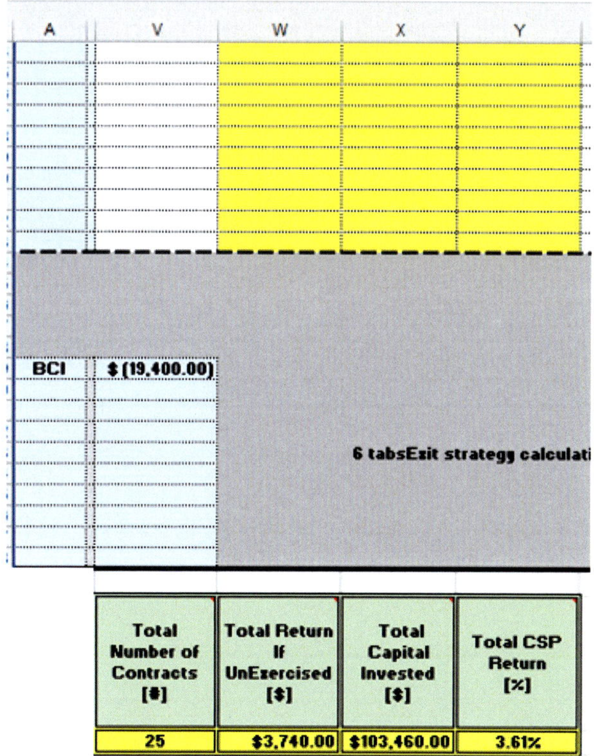

Figure 117: Close-up Views of the Capital Adjustment Section

Discussion

When using multiple exit strategies in the same contract cycle, we must first close the initial adjusted trade. The second-income stream trade is entered *in another row* and a *capital adjustment subtraction is entered* in Column V (Total Capital Invested) directly below the 2nd trade calculations. This will ensure accuracy of the total capital invested in each contract cycle and allow for credible total portfolio % returns.

Chapter 27

The PCP (Put-Call-Put) Strategy

Combining cash-secured puts and covered call writing

What is the PCP strategy?

This is a multi-tiered option-selling strategy, sometimes referred to as the *wheel strategy* outside the BCI community, where an OTM cash-secured put is sold and, if exercised and shares are *put* to us, a covered call is written on those underlying shares. The strike of the covered call can be OTM (more aggressive) or ITM (more defensive). If and when the short call is exercised and shares are sold, the cash is then used to secure another put sale. *The PCP strategy can be considered to be an exit plan for both covered call writing and selling cash-secured puts.*

Graphic representation of the PCP strategy

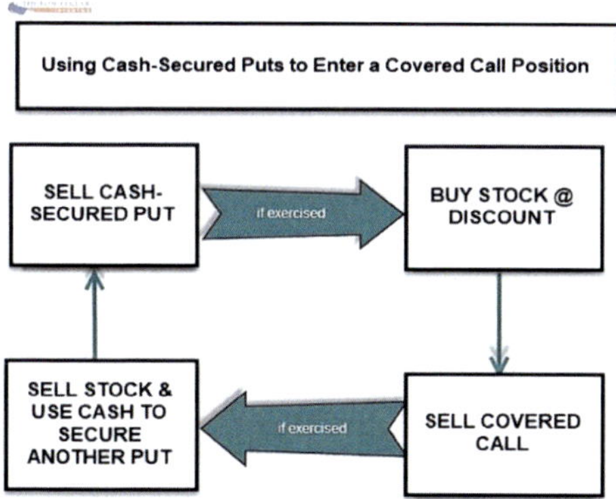

Figure 118: Combining Covered Call Writing and Selling Cash-Secured Puts

When to consider the PCP strategy

I believe that PCP is appropriate in all market conditions depending on strategy goals and personal risk-tolerance. That said, it is particularly useful in volatile and bear market conditions as demonstrated with this real-life example with T-Mobile US Inc. (Nasdaq: TMUS). We will sell an OTM cash-secured put and then review the OTM and ITM covered call strikes.

Real-life example with TMUS

- 4/7/2020: TMUS is trading at $86.09
- 4/7/2020: STO 1 x 5/15/2020 $82.50 OTM put at $2.91
- 5/15/2020: The $82.50 put expires ITM and shares are *put* to us at $82.50 (less the $2.91 put premium) for a breakeven price point of $79.59
- 5/18/2020: Consider the 6/19/2020 OTM $82.50 call strike
- 5/18/2020: Consider the 6/19/2020 ITM $77.50 call strike

Initial put trade entries

Stock Symbol	Industry	Entry Trade Date	ER Date	Ex Div Date	Entry Trade Expiry Date	Entry Stock Price [$/sh]	Entry Put Strike Price [$]	Entry Put Option Price [$/sh]	# Shares
TMUS	Telecom	4/07/20	06/20/20	06/26/20	05/15/20	$ 86.09	$ 82.50	$ 2.91	100

Figure 119: TMUS: Entering Our Initial Put Trade

Initial put trade returns

Expected # Of Days In Trade [#]	Time Value [$/sh]	Premium Collected Per Contract [$]	Cash Req/Cont [$]	Breakeven [$/sh]	Return On Option ROO [%]	Return On Option ROO Annual'zd [%]	ROO Premium [$]	Purchase Discount If Exercised [%]	Stock Cost/Share If Exercised [$/sh]	Total Capital Invested n [$]
39	$ 2.91	$ 291.00	$ 7,959.00	$ 79.59	3.66%	34.22%	$ 291.00	7.55%	$ 79.59	$ 7,959.00

Figure 120: TMUS: Initial Put Trade Returns

The initial return on the put option sale is 3.66%, 34.22% annualized based on a 39-day trade. Shares are *put* to us if the strike moves ITM at expiration and we take no action to close the ITM short put. TMUS is purchased at a breakeven price point of $79.59 or a 7.55% discount from the share price when the put sale was initiated.

Initial covered call trade entries using ITM ($77.50) and OTM ($82.50) strikes

Stock Symbol	Industry	Entry Trade Date	ER Date	Ex-Div Date	Entry Trade Expiry Date	Entry Stock Price [$/sh]	Entry Call Strike Price [$]	Entry Call Option Premium [$/sh]	Number Of Shares [#]
TMUS	Telecom	05/18/20	06/20/20	06/26/20	06/19/20	$ 79.59	$ 82.50	$ 2.30	100
TMUS	Telecom	05/18/20	06/20/20	06/26/20	06/19/20	$ 79.59	$ 77.50	$ 4.25	100

Figure 121: TMUS: Entering Our Initial Covered Call Trade

The ITM $77.50 strike is a more defensive approach to the covered call writing leg of the strategy, while the OTM $82.50 strike implies a more aggressive objective.

Initial covered call returns for ITM and OTM strikes

OPENING TRADE								
Expected # Of Days In Trade [#]	Time-Value Per-Share [$/sh]	Intrinsic-Value Per-Share [$/sh]	Upside Value Per-Share [$/sh]	Breakeven Value Per-Share [$/sh]	Return On Option ROO [%]	Return On Option ROO Annual'zd [%]	Upside Potential [%]	Downside Protect. [%]
33	$ 2.30	$ -	$ 2.91	$ 77.29	2.89%	31.96%	3.66%	0.00%
33	$ 2.16	$ 2.09	$ -	$ 75.34	2.79%	30.83%	0.00%	2.63%

Trade ROO Premium [$]	Trade Upside Premium [$]	Total Capital Invested [$]
$ 230.00	$ 291.00	$ 7,959.00
$ 216.00	$ -	$ 7,750.00

Figure 122: TMUS: Initial Covered Call Trade Returns

Downside PCP protection on steroids

Expected # Of Days In Trade [#]	Time Value [$/sh]	Premium Collected Per Contract [$]	Cash Req/Cont [$]	Breakeven [$/sh]	Return On Option ROO [%]	Return On Option ROO Annual'zd [%]	ROO Premium [$]	Purchase Discount If Exercised [%]	Stock Cost/Share If Exercised [$/sh]	Total Capital Invested n [$]
39	$ 2.91	$ 291.00	$ 7,959.00	$ 79.59	3.66%	34.22%	$ 291.00	7.55%	$ 79.59	$ 7,959.00

OPENING TRADE											
Expected # Of Days In Trade [#]	Time-Value Per-Share [$/sh]	Intrinsic-Value Per-Share [$/sh]	Upside Value Per-Share [$/sh]	Breakeven Value Per-Share [$/sh]	Return On Option ROO [%]	Return On Option ROO Annual'zd [%]	Upside Potential [%]	Down Protect. [%]	Trade ROO Premium [$]	Trade Upside Premium [$]	Total Capital Invested [$]
33	$ 2.30	$ -	$ 2.91	$ 77.29	2.89%	31.96%	3.66%	0.00%	$ 230.00	$ 291.00	$ 7,959.00
33	$ 2.16	$ 2.09	$	$ 75.34	2.79%	30.83%	0.00%	2.63%	$ 216.00	$ -	$ 7,750.00

Figure 123: Put-Selling and Covered Call Writing Combined Results

Downside protection to breakeven

- Put trade: 7.55%
- Call trade for the ITM $77.50 strike: 5.3%
- Total 72-day downside protection: 12.85%

Combining covered call writing and selling cash-secured puts into one multi-tiered option selling strategy, where each approach can serve as an exit strategy for the other, will provide substantial protection to the downside especially in bear and volatile market conditions.

I also believe that PCP is an outstanding game plan for all market conditions.

Discussion

The goal of the PCP strategy is to generate cash-flow. Each leg of the trade will accomplish either premium returns or purchasing a stock at a discount. Since there is a breakeven price point associated with each leg of the trade, there is risk that share value can decline below that price and we can start to lose money. This is one of the main reasons I am writing this book to provide us with the tools necessary to mitigate losses, enhance gains and turn losses into gains.

Note: A *protective put* can be added to the covered call trade thereby converting the covered call trade to a *collar trade*. Detailing this strategy is beyond the scope of this book but a general overview will be presented:

- Buy BCI at $48.00 (long stock)

- Sell an OTM $50.00 call at $2.00 (Add short call; now a covered call trade and places a ceiling on the trade)
- Buy an OTM protective put at $1.00 (add a long put; now a collar trade and places a floor on the trade)

The maximum gain is the $1.00 net option credit + share gain from $48.00 to the OTM $50.00 call strike ($3.00/$48.00 = 6.25%)

The maximum loss is the $1.00 net option credit minus the maximum share loss of $3.00 ($48.00 - $45.00) for a total net loss of $-2.00 (-$2.00/$48.00 = -4.16%). The long put protects against catastrophic loss to the downside at the expense of a lower net option return.

See the BCI book, Covered call Writing Alternative Strategies, for detailed information on the collar trade.

Appendix I
Additional Educational Products

www.thebluecollarinvestor.com/store

Books

- *The Complete Encyclopedia for Covered Call Writing-classic 3rd Edition*
- *The Complete Encyclopedia for Covered call Writing-Volume 2*
- *Selling Cash-Secured Puts*
- *Covered Call Writing Alternative Strategies*
- *Stock Investing for Students*

Online Video Lessons with Downloadable Workbooks

- *Covered Call Writing Package*
- *Selling Cash-Secured Puts Basic & Advanced Principles*
- *The Collar Strategy*
- *Portfolio Overwriting*

- *The Poor Man's Covered Call*
- *Stock Investing for Students: 12-Part Financial Literacy Program*
- *Exit Strategies for Covered Call Writing*
- *Complete Streaming Video Bundle*
- *Covered Call Writing Alternative Strategy Bundle*

Calculators & Spreadsheets

- *Trade Management System with the Trade Management Calculator*
- *Elite Plus Calculator*
- *Elite Put-Selling Calculator*
- *Poor Man's Covered call (PMCC) Calculator*
- *Portfolio Overwriting Calculator*
- *Stock Repair Calculator*
- *Calculator Bundle Package*
- *Trade Planner*
- *Collar Calculator*

Premium Membership

- *Weekly Stock Reports published on before market opens on Monday (usually Sat. or Sun.)*
- *Weekly Exchange-Traded Funds Reports published mid-week, usually Wednesdays*
- *Quarterly High Dividend Yield Stocks with LEAPS Reports for dividend capture strategies*
- *Monthly Blue Chip (Dow 30) Portfolio Reports*
- *Dozens of resources and download files*

1-on-1 Coaching Program

- *https://www.thebluecollarinvestor.com/investment-coach/*

Free Resources

- *https://www.thebluecollarinvestor.com/free-resources/*
- *https://www.thebluecollarinvestor.com/beginners-corner/*
- *https://www.thebluecollarinvestor.com/beginners-corner-puts-selling/*

- *https://www.thebluecollarinvestor.com/blog/*

BCI Package: Our Best and Most Comprehensive Investment Package

- *https://thebluecollarinvestor.com/minimembership/bci-investor-program/*

Appendix II
Testimonials

Hi Alan,
I've read and watched YouTube's by many people who purport to utilize option selling programs. What is exceptional about what you do is the way you document your articles. It's almost like reading a synopsis of a medical case. Regardless of what approach one does, being highly organized is very important, IMO.
Best regards,
David

Hi Alan,
I've been a BCI member for about 3 months. I was already comfortable with the technical and fundamental side of stocks. For me learning options was a different animal, I couldn't grasp the concept easily. I tried studying a few other online teachers and was ready to give up when someone suggested your site. I spend 15-20 hours a week reading your books and online streaming. You have a lot of material to learn from which is great, but a person has to put in the time to study. The end of Feb. or beginning of March, I will be ready to make my first option trades. I'm very excited but wish markets were better. So, thanks to your style of clarity and teaching, options make a lot of sense to me now. Keep teaching so we can keep learning.
Stan

{YouTube comment}
Dr. Ellman and BCI are the best and most complete authority on the strategy of making money on selling covered calls and

cash secured puts. While I have actually performed this "rolling-in" strategy ion the past, Alan Ellman's discussion and his and his team's putting together a detailed precise strategy is something that I never would have done. Kudos! My experience with equity options now spans 5 decades. Excellent job Alan and thank you.

Ronald

Good morning Dr. Ellman,
First, I'd like to express my gratitude and appreciation for everything you have taught me. It has been a great experience for me these past few months. I've learned as I went along every step of the way, Now, my mind is full of strategies and how-to's. I feel in control of my investing.
I can't thank you enough for the book and knowledge you have shared with me and, likely, countless others.

Sincerely,
George

Dear Alan,
I can't say enough good things about Vol *1 and 2, and the Exit Strategies booklet.*

I want to share my success with you over just the last few weeks.
Like many investors, I had a portfolio of ''buy and hold' stocks but was unaware of covered call writing.

I have earned in excess of $6k in option premiums and almost $3k on max profit assignments in 70 days.

My Return on initial investment is 17.05%
Annualized at 90.26%.

My only disappointment is that I was not aware of covered call writing much sooner.

And a warning to new covered call writers…it's a bit addicting!

All my best,
Joe

Hi Alan,
Another fantastic month. $2563 profit for the expiration cycle ending on 11/19!

Thanks again for your terrific service. The Weekly Stock Screener along with the BCI Elite-Plus Calculator have proven to be invaluable.

Bruce (NY)

Appendix III
Data Entry and Calculated Result Index

COVERED CALLS				
Initial Trade Entry Data - Calls		Column		Entry/Result Unit
Stock Symbol		A		Alpha.
Industry		B		Alpha.
Entry Trade Date		C		mm/dd/yy
Earnings Report (ER) Date		D		mm/dd/yy
Ex Dividend (Ex- Div) Date		E		mm/dd/yy
Entry Trade Expiry Date		F		mm/dd/yy
Entry Stock Price		G		$/Share
Entry Call Strike Price		H		$
Entry Call Option Premium		i		$/Share
Number Of Shares		J		#
Entry Calculated Results - Calls				
Expected # Of Days in Trade		L		#
Time-Value Per-Share		M		$/Share
Intrinsic-Value Per-Share		N		$/Share
Upside Value Per-Share		O		$/Share
Breakeven Value Per-Share		p		$/Share
Return On Option (ROO)		Q		%
Return On Option (ROO) Annualized		R		%
Upside Potential		S		%
Downside Protect.		T		%
Trade ROO Premium		U		$
Trade Upside Premium		V		$
Total Capital Invested		W		$
20% Option Exit Guideline		X		$
10% Option Exit Guideline		Y		$
7% Stock Exit Guideline		Z		$
Target Entry Monthly Trade Portfolio Results - Calls				
Total Number Of Contracts		T85		#
Initial Option Return		U85		$
Potential Upside Return		V85		$
Total Target Return (ROO+Upside)		W85		$

Total Capital Invested		X85		$
Return Flat (ROO)		Y85		%
Total Potential (ROO+Upside) Return		Z85		%
Trade Exit/Adjustment Data - Calls				
Stock Symbol (Carried Over From Col. A)		AB		Alpha.
Exit Strategy Selected (From Dropdown Menu)		AC		Alpha.
Adjust. Trade Date		AD		mm/dd/yy
Adjust. Expiry Date		AE		mm/dd/yy
BTC Entry Option Price		AF		$/Share
STO Entry #2 Strike Price		AG		$
STO Entry #2 Option Premium		AH		$/Share
Final Stock Sale Price If Sold		AI		$/Share
Final Unsold Stock Price		AJ		$/Share
Trade Exit/Adjustment Calculated Results - Calls				
Final Net Option Profit/Loss		AK		$/Share
Final Net Option Profit/Loss		AL		$
Final Net Option Return		AM		%
Realized Final Stock Profit/Loss per share		AN		$/Share
Realized Final $ Total Stock Profit/Loss		AO		$
Realized Final Stock Profit/Loss		AP		%
Unrealized Final Stock Profit/Loss		AQ		$/Share
Unrealized Final Stock $ Total Stock Profit/Loss		AR		$
Unreal. Final Stock % Total Stock Profit/Loss		AS		%
Combined Final Trade Total Profit/Loss		AU		$
Combined Final Trade Total Profit/Loss		AV		%
Final Monthly Trade Portfolio Results - Calls				
Total Number Of Contracts		AP85		#
Net Option Value		AQ85		$
Total Final Realized Stock Profit/Loss		AR85		$
Total Final Unrealized Stock Profit/Loss		AS85		$
Net Portfolio Final Position Value		AU85		$
Net Portfolio Final Position Return		AV85		%
CASH SECURED PUTS				
Initial Trade Entry Data - Puts		Column		Entry/Result Unit
Stock Symbol		A		Alpha.
Industry		B		Alpha.
Entry Trade Date		C		mm/dd/yy
Earnings Report (ER) Date		D		mm/dd/yy
Ex Dividend (Ex-Div Date)		E		mm/dd/yy
Entry Trade Expiry Date		F		mm/dd/yy

Entry Stock Price		G		$/Share
Entry Put Strike Price		H		$
Entry PUT Option Premium		i		$/Share
Number Of Shares		J		#
Entry Calculated Results - Puts				
Expected # Of Days In Trade		L		#
Time-Value Per-Share		M		$/Share
Put Premium Collected Per Share Contract		N		$
Cash Req/Contract		O		$
Breakeven Value Per-Share		p		$/Share
Return On Option (ROO)		Q		%
Return On Option (ROO) Annualized		R		%
ROO Premium		S		$
Purchase Discount If Exercised		T		%
Stock Cost/Share If Exercised		U		$/Share
Total Capital Invested		V		$
3% Stock Exit Guideline		W		$
20% Option Exit Guideline		X		$
10% Stock Exit Guideline		Y		$
Target Entry Monthly Trade Portfolio Results - Puts				
Total Number Of Contracts		V162		#
Total Return If Unexercised		W162		$
Total Capital Invested		X162		$
Total CSP Return		Y162		%
Trade Exit/Adjustment Data - Puts				
Stock Symbol (Carried Over From Col. A)		AB		Alpha.
Exit Strategy Selected (From Dropdown Menu)		AC		Alpha.
Adjust. Trade Date		AD		mm/dd/yy
Adjust. Expiry Date		AE		mm/dd/yy
BTC Entry Option Price		AF		$/Share
STO Entry #2 Strike Price		AG		$/Share
STO Entry #2 Option Premium		AH		$/Share
Current Stock Price Basis		AI		$
Price of Stock At Time of Exercise		AJ		$
Trade Exit/Adjustment Calculated Results - Puts				
Final Net Option Profit/Loss		AK		$/Share
Final Net Option Profit/Loss		AL		$
Final Net Option Return		AM		%
Unrealized Final Stock Profit/Loss		AN		$
Unrealized Final Stock $ Total Stock Profit/Loss		AO		$
Unreal. Final Stock % Total Stock Profit/Loss		AP		%

Combined Final Trade Total Profit/Loss		AQ		$
Combined Final Trade Total Profit/Loss		AR		%
Final Monthly Trade Portfolio Results - Puts				
Total Number Of Contracts		AN162		#
Final Net Option Value		AO162		$
Unrealized Final Stock Profit/Loss		AP162		$
Net Final Return Value		AQ162		$
Net Portfolio Final Position Return		AR162		%

Appendix IV
Explanation of Rolling-Out Trade Entries & Calculations

Overview

When rolling-out a covered call trade, we close the current month ITM short call and sell a later-dated covered call while still retaining the underlying shares. The trades can be rolled-out to the same strike or out-and-up to a higher strike which can be ITM, ATM or OTM compared to current market value of the underlying security. This creates a dilemma as how to enter and calculate these trades over 2 different time frames.

When using the BCI Trade Management Calculator (TMC) or a manual trading log, here is how we break down the calculations and entries over a 2-month time frame (other time frames work as well):

Current month

- Initial call premium is entered and become realized income if the strike expires ITM
- Final share value at expiration is the ITM strike as this is the highest value our shares can be worth due to our contractual obligation to sell at that price
- The current month trade is closed at the maximum gain

Later-dated month
The stock entry price is the previous month's ITM strike

The option premium entered is the later-dated option premium minus the cost-to-close the current month premium

This information is entered into a new page in our trade journal TMC)

Hypothetical example

3/21/2022: Buy 100 x BCI at $48.00

3/21/2022: STO 1 4/15/2022 $50.00 call at $1.50

4/15/2022: BCI trading at $52.00 as expiration approaches, leaving the $50.00 strike ITM

4/15/2022: Shares can be worth no more than $50.00 due to the contract obligation to sell at that price and entered as the final unrealized share value

4/15/2022: The $50.00 share value is transferred to the next contract page of the TMC or manual trading log

4/15/2022: BTC the 4/15/2022 $50.00 call at $2.10

4/15/2022: STO the 5/20/2022 $50.00 call (roll-out) at $3.75

4/15/2022: The net option credit is entered as $1.65

Key

- Yellow field: Current month
- Green field: Next contract month

TMC entries & calculations: current month

Initial trade entries

Stock Symbol	Industry	Entry Trade Date	ER Date	Ex-Div Date	Entry Trade Expiry Date	Entry Stock Price [$/sh]	Entry Call Strike Price [$]	Entry Call Option Premium [$/sh]	Number Of Shares [#]
BCI		03/21/22			04/15/22	$ 48.00	$ 50.00	$ 1.50	100

Initial trade calculations

OPENING TRADE											
Expected # Of Days In Trade [#]	Time-Value Per-Share [$/sh]	Intrinsic-Value Per-Share [$/sh]	Upside Value Per-Share [$/sh]	Breakeven Value Per-Share [$/sh]	Return On Option ROO [%]	Return On Option ROO Annual'zd [%]	Upside Potential [%]	Downside Protect. [%]	Trade ROO Premium [$]	Trade Upside Premium [$]	Total Capital Invested [$]
26	$ 1.50	$ -	$ 2.00	$ 46.50	3.13%	43.87%	4.17%	0.00%	$ 150.00	$ 200.00	$ 4,800.00

Rolling-out trade adjustments in current month

Stock Symbol	Exit Strategy Selected	Adjust. Trade Date	Adjust. Expiry Date	BTC Entry Option Price [$/Sh]	STO Entry #2 Strike Price [$]	STO Entry #2 Option Premium [$/Sh]	Final Stock Sale Price If Sold [$/Sh]	Final Unsold Stock Price [$/Sh]
BCI	Roll-Out	04/15/22						$ 50.00

Final results in current month showing maximum return

Final Net Option Profit/Loss [$/Sh]	Final Net Option Profit/Loss [$]	Final Net Option Return [%]	Realized Final Stock Profit/Loss per share [$/Sh]	Realized Final $ Total Stock Profit/Loss [$]	Realized Final Stock Profit/Loss [%]	Unrealized Final Stock Profit/Loss [$/Sh]	Unrealized Final Stock $ Total Stock Profit/Loss [$]	Unreal. Final Stock % Total Stock Profit/Loss [%]	Combined Final Trade Total Profit/Loss [$]	Combined Final Trade Total Profit/Loss [%]
$ 1.50	$ 150.00	3.13%	$ -	$ -	-	$ 2.00	$ 200.00	4.17%	$ 350.00	7.29%

TMC entries & calculations: next, later-dated month

Initial trade entries (month #2)

Stock Symbol	Industry	Entry Trade Date	ER Date	Ex-Div Date	Entry Trade Expiry Date	Entry Stock Price [$/sh]	Entry Call Strike Price [$]	Entry Call Option Premium [$/sh]	Number Of Shares [#]
BCI		04/15/22			05/20/22	$ 50.00	$ 50.00	$ 1.65	100

Initial trade calculations (month #2)

Expected # Of Days In Trade [#]	Time-Value Per-Share [$/sh]	Intrinsic-Value Per-Share [$/sh]	Upside Value Per-Share [$/sh]	Breakeven Value Per-Share [$/sh]	Return On Option ROO [%]	Return On Option ROO Annual'zd [%]	Upside Potential [%]	Downside Protect. [%]	Trade ROO Premium [$]	Trade Upside Premium [$]	Total Capital Invested [$]
36	$ 1.65	$ -	$ -	$ 48.35	3.30%	33.46%	0.00%	0.00%	$ 165.00	$ -	$ 5,000.00

Discussion

When rolling-out an ITM strike, the final unrealized share value is entered as the ITM strike price and the current month trade is closed at the maximum gain.

The rolled-out trade is entered into the next page of the TMC for the later-dated contracts, using the ITM strike as the entered stock price and the option value as the net credit or debit of the new premium (later-dated option) minus the cost-to-close premium (current month BTC premium).

Glossary

Accumulation: Buying of stock by institutional or professional investors over an extended period of time.

Acquisition: When one company purchases the majority interest in the acquired.

Actively Managed Mutual Funds: Shareholders, through a mutual fund manager, buy and sell stocks and bonds, within the fund, in an attempt to *beat the market*.

Advance-Decline Theory: Also called the *Breadth of Market Theory,* this theory states that the market direction can be determined by the number of stocks that have increased compared to those that have decreased in value. It is considered bullish if more shares are advancing than declining.

American Depository Receipt: A negotiable certificate issued by a U.S. bank representing a specified number of shares (or one share) in a foreign stock that is traded on a U.S. exchange. ADRs are denominated in U.S. dollars, with the underlying security held by a U.S. financial institution overseas. ADRs help to reduce administration and duty costs that would otherwise be levied on each transaction.

American Style Options: An option contract that may be exercised at any time between the date of purchase and the expiration date.

Arbitrage: The simultaneous purchase and sale of an asset in order to profit from a difference in the price. It is a trade that profits by exploiting price differences of identical or similar financial instruments, on different markets or in different forms.

Ask: The price a seller is willing to accept for a security. It includes both price and quantity willing to be sold.

Asset allocation: The implementation of an investment strategy that attempts to balance risk versus reward by adjusting the percentage of each asset in an investment portfolio according to the investor's risk tolerance, goals and investment time frame

Assignment: The receipt of an exercise notice by an option seller that obligates him to sell (in the case of a call) or purchase (in the case of a put) the underlying security at the specified strike price.

At-the-money: An option is at-the-money if the strike price of the option is equal to the market price of the underlying security.

Balance sheet: One of the major financial statements used by accountants and business owners. (The other major financial statements are the income statement, statement of cash flows, and statement of stockholders' equity) The balance sheet is also referred to as the **statement of financial position.** The balance sheet presents a company's financial position at the end of a specified date.

Banned stocks: According to the BCI methodology, this is a list of stocks that should be avoided at all times when selling short-term options because of risky monthly reports.

Bar Chart: This price chart consists of session high and lows as well as the opening and closing prices. It is also referred to as the O-H-L-C bar.

Basis: Basis is often a moving target. Generally, it is what you paid for a stock or option. There are adjustments which may be necessary to report the proper capital gain. These adjustments may include special dividends, stock splits and stock dividends, and some others.

Bear put spread: A bear put spread is a vertical options strategy that is used when the investor believes that the price of a stock will most likely decline. Bear Put Spread is constructed by purchasing put options at a specific strike price while also selling the same number of puts at a lower strike price, in most cases one strike below the purchased put.

Bearish: Pessimistic investor sentiment that a particular security or market is headed downward.

Benchmark: A standard against which the performance of a security, mutual fund or investment manager can be measured. A common example is the S&P 500.

Beta: This is a measure of the volatility or *systemic risk* (market risk) of a security as compared to the market as a whole.

Bid: An offer made by an investor to buy an equity. It will include price and quantity.

Bid-Ask Spread: The difference in price between the highest price that a buyer is willing to pay for the option and the lowest price a seller is willing to sell it.

Black-Scholes Option Pricing Model: A model used to calculate the value of an option, by factoring in stock price, strike price and expiration date, risk-free return, and the standard deviation of the stock's return.

Blue chip: A blue chip is a nationally recognized, well-established and financially sound company. Blue chips generally sell high-quality, widely accepted products and services which helps to contribute to their long record of stable and reliable growth.

Breakeven: The point at which gains equal losses.

Brokerage statement: A broker's statement is a monthly snapshot of a brokerage account activity.

Bullish: Optimistic investor sentiment that a particular equity or market will rise.

Buy and hold portfolio: This is an investment strategy where an investor buys stocks and holds them for a long time.

Buy down price of stock: Using the intrinsic value of an in-the-money option premium to reduce the cost of the stock purchase.

Buy to close: A term used by many brokerages to represent the closing of a short position in option transactions.

Buy-write combination form: A brokerage trading form that allows for the simultaneous purchase of an underlying security and the sale of a corresponding call option resulting in a net debit limit order.

Buy-write order: See net debit order

Calendar Spread- Simultaneously establishing long and short options positions on the same underlying stock with different expiration dates. For example, you buy the December 2017 $20 call and sell the April, 2017 $20 call on the same equity. Also referred to as a Horizontal or Time Spread.

Call: An option contract giving the owner the right (but not the obligation) to buy a specified amount of an underlying security at a specified price within a specified time.

Campaign collar: Also known as a Long-Term Collar. Collar strategy where the investor is planning to hold the stock for a longer period of time or trading a long-term portfolio holding. When trading a stock in your long-term portfolio, using a long term put will provide the protection while also providing incremental income from the near-term call.

Candlestick Chart*:* This chart is created by displaying the high, low, open and close for a security each day over a certain time frame.

Capacity report: A monthly report on trends in the supply of airline flights and seats.

Capital Asset: This is pretty much anything you own and use for personal, pleasure or investment purposes. The term includes such tangible assets as a boat, a coin collection, or a piece of real estate. It may also include intangible assets, such as a patent or copyright. The distinction between a capital asset and a non-capital asset is its use. Any capital asset becomes a non-capital asset if it is used in a trade or business, or is "for sale" to customers in a trade or business.

Capital Gain (Loss): A capital gain or loss is simply the difference between the proceeds of the sale and your cost basis of the asset sold. If you bought a stock for $25 and sold it for $30, you have a capital gain of $5. You can't have a capital gain or loss unless you have a sale of a capital asset. However, a sale of an asset does not necessarily mean you have a capital gain or loss. Why... because every capital gain requires two parts of the transaction, a sale AND an acquisition, or purchase.

Capital risk: The risk an investor faces that he or she may lose all or part of the principal amount invested.

Cash account: A regular brokerage account in which the customer is required by Regulation T to pay for securities within two days of the purchase.

Cash-secured put: When a brokerage company requires us to have the cash in our accounts to purchase the shares we are obligated to buy after selling a put option.

Cash settlement: A settlement method used in certain future and option contracts whereby, upon expiration or exercise, the seller of the financial instrument does not deliver shares but transfers the associated cash position.

CBOE S&P 500 BuyWrite Index (BXM): This is a benchmark index designed to track the performance of a hypothetical buy-write strategy on the S&P 500 Index.

CBOE Volatility Index: see VIX

Collar (strategy): A protective options strategy that is implemented after a long position in a stock has experienced substantial gains. It is created by purchasing an out of the money put option while simultaneously writing an out of the money call option.

Compound calculator: An interest calculator used to quantify the impact compound interest has on the future value of an asset.

Compound interest: Interest calculated on the initial principal and also on the accumulated interest of previous periods of a deposit or loan. Compound interest can be thought of as "interest on interest"

Compounding: The ability of an asset to generate earnings, which are then reinvested in order to generate earnings of their own.

Consolidation: Sideways Pattern (consolidation/ - the horizontal price movement of an equity where the forces of supply and demand are equal. The stock simply cannot establish an uptrend or a downtrend.

Contract adjustment: Changes to option contract terms due to underlying corporate actions like stock splits or special cash dividends.

Contract cycle: The period of time starting with the first trading day after expiration Friday through the end of the following expiration Friday (4 PM EST unless there is an exchange recognized holiday).

Convert Dead Money to Cash Profits: An exit strategy wherein an option is bought back and the underlying equity sold. The cash is then used to buy a better performing stock which is used to sell another covered call.

Correlation*:* This measures the degree to which investments are related.

Cost basis: The original value of an asset. It is used to determine the capital gain, which is equal to the difference between the asset's cost basis and the current market value. Also: the amount of your original investment.

Cost to carry: When money is borrowed from our broker in a margin account, interest is charged and needs to be calculated into our results.

Covered call ETF: An exchange-traded fund that uses covered call writing as its primary income-producing vehicle.

Covered call writing: A strategy in which one sells call options while simultaneously owning the underlying security.

Covered combination: A strategy in options trading that involves selling equal number of out-of-the-money calls and puts on the same underlying security, strike price and expiration date while owning the underlying stock.

Covered put: A bearish options strategy involving the writing of put options while shorting the obligated shares of the underlying stock.

Credit Collar: Protective collar that results in a credit after the put is purchased and the call is sold. Also, the condition for a collar trade where the premium for selling the call is greater than the premium cost of the put.

Currency carry trade: A strategy in which an investor sells a certain currency with a relatively low interest rate and uses the funds to purchase a different currency yielding a higher interest rate. A trader using this strategy attempts to capture the difference between the rates, which can often be substantial, depending on the amount of leverage the investor chooses to use.

Debit collar: Protective collar that results in a debit after the put is purchased and the call is sold. Also, the condition for a collar trade where the premium for selling the call is less than the premium cost of the put.

Delta: This is the amount an option value will change for every $1 change in the price of a stock. Another definition is that the delta value indicates the probability that the option strike ends up in-the-money at expiration. Delta values for calls run from 0 to 1. For Puts, 0 to-1.

Derivative: A security whose price is dependent upon or derived from one or more underlying assets. The derivative itself is merely a contract between two or more parties. Its value is determined by fluctuations in the underlying asset. The most common underlying assets include stocks, bonds, commodities, currencies, interest rates and market indexes. Most derivatives are characterized by high leverage.

Diagonal Spread- A long and short options position with different expirations AND strikes. For example, you buy the December, 2010 $20 call and sell the April, 2010 $25 call.

Dilution: A reduction in earnings per share of common stock that occurs through the issuance of additional shares. This is avoided with stock splits by reducing the current market value of a stock by a similar ratio as was the number of shares increased.

Distribution: the selling of stock by large institutions over an extending period of time.

Diversification: A risk management technique that mixes a wide variety of investments within a portfolio. The rationale behind this technique contends that a portfolio of different kinds of investments will, on average, yield higher returns and pose a lower risk than any individual investment found within the portfolio.

Dividend: A distribution of a portion of a company's earnings to a class of its shareholders as cash payments or shares of stock.

Dollar cost averaging: The technique of buying a fixed dollar amount of a particular investment on a regular schedule, regardless of the share price. More shares are purchased when prices are low, and fewer shares are bought when prices are high.

Downside protection: The intrinsic value portion of an in-the-money call option premium divided by the original cost of the underlying stock. It is the percentage of your investment that can be lost without affecting the option return on your investment. The formula is as follows:

$$\frac{\text{Intrinsic Value of option premium}}{\text{Original Cost of stock}} = \text{\% of downside protection}$$

Down trending Stock: A stock with a declining share price showing lower highs and lower lows.

The Dow Theory: This theory states that the market is in an upward trend if one of the averages (industrial or transportation) advances above a previous significant high and is accompanied by a similar advance in the other. A major trend is identified only when BOTH the Dow Industrial and Dow Transportation Averages reach a new high or a new low. Without this confirmation, the market will return to its previous trading pattern.

Dynamic Collar: Collar strategy which uses puts and calls that are more than a month in duration (typically two to three months or more). Here the put is purchased two or more months out while front month short calls are sold against the longer term put.

Early exercise (assignment): Early exercise happens when the owner of a call or put invokes his or her contractual rights before expiration. As a result, an option seller will be assigned and shares of stock will change hands.
Earnings estimate: An analyst's estimate for a company's future quarterly or annual earnings.

Earnings guidance: Information that a company provides as an indication or estimate of their future earnings.

Earnings per share: A company's profit divided by the number of common outstanding shares.

Earnings report: A quarterly filing made by public companies to report their performance. Included in these reports are items such as net income, earnings per share, earnings from continuing operations, and net sales. These reports follow the end of each quarter. Most companies file in January, April, July, and October.

Earnings surprise: When the earnings reported in a company's quarterly or annual report are above or below analysts' earnings estimates.

Efficient frontier: A line created from the risk-reward graph, comprised of optimal portfolios.

Elite Calculator: Expanded version of the basic Ellman Calculator (ESOC) which includes an *unwind tab* and a *Schedule D.*

Ellman Calculator: An Excel calculator used to compute covered call writing option returns. The spreadsheet includes time value return on option (ROO), upside potential when selling out-of-the-money calls and downside protection of initial time value profit when selling in-the-money calls. There is also a breakeven column.

ETFs: See exchange traded funds.

Exchange traded funds: A security that tracks an index, a commodity, or a basket of assets like an index fund, but trades like a stock on an exchange, thus experiencing price changes throughout the day as it is bought and sold. These securities provide the diversification of an index fund.

Ex-dividend date: The trading day before the ex-dividend date is the last day one must own shares of stock to be eligible to collect an announced dividend. If you buy the shares on the ex-dividend date, you will not receive the dividend.

Exercise: To Exercise an option means to put into effect the right specified in a Call or Put option. The owner, purchaser, or option holder of a call (put) option has the right, but not the obligation, to buy (sell) the underlying stock at a specified strike price by a specified date.

Exercise notice: A broker's notification that a client wishes to exercise his or her right to buy or sell the underlying security. The exercise notice is forwarded to the option seller via the Options Clearing Corporation.

Expiration cycle: The pattern of months in which options contracts expire.

European Style Option: An option contract that can only be exercised on the expiration date.

Execution (of a trade): The completion of a buy or sell stock order.

Exit strategy: A plan in which a trader intends to get out of an investment position made in the past. Cashing out is a complete exit strategy. Closing out of a position maybe a partial or a complete exit strategy.

Expanded Weekly options: Options that are listed to provide expiration opportunities every week. Weeklys are typically listed on Thursdays and expire on Fridays, provided that such expirations were not previously listed. Expanded Weeklys can be traded weeks in advance.

Expected Return*:* Possible return on a portfolio in different market conditions (bullish, bearish and neutral) weighted by the likelihood that the return will occur.

Expense ratio: A measure of what it costs an investment company to operate a mutual fund. It is determined through an annual calculation, where a fund's operating expenses are divided by the average dollar value of its managed assets Operating expenses are taken out of a fund's assets and lower the return to a fund's investors. Some funds have a marketing cost referred to as a 12b-1 fee, which would also be included in operating expenses. It is interesting that a fund's trading activity - the buying and selling of stock - is NOT included in the calculation of expense ratio.

Expiration Friday(date): The last day (in the case of an American- style) or the only day (in the case of European-style) on which an option may be exercised. For stock options, this date is the third Friday of the expiration month. If Friday is a holiday, the last trading day is the preceding Thursday.

Exponential moving average or EMA: A type of moving average that is similar to a simple moving average, except that more weight is given to the most recent data. It reacts faster to recent price changes than does a simple moving average. The 12- and 26-day EMA's are the most popular short-term averages, and they are used to create indicators like the MACD.

FIFO: See First in, first out.

Financial statement: A collection of reports about an organization's financial results, financial condition, and cash flows

First call: A company that gathers research notes and earnings estimates from brokerage analysts and forms a consensus estimate. The estimate is compared to the actual earnings reports, and then the difference between the two is the earnings surprise. The other major player in this estimate game is **Zachs.**

First in, first out: An asset-management and valuation method in which the assets produced or acquired first are then sold first.

Fundamental analysis: A method of analyzing the prospects of a security by observing the accepted accounting measures such as earnings, sales, and assets and so on.

Future delivery price: The financial value of the underlying security or commodity when a futures contract expires.

Gamma: The rate of change for delta with respect to the price of the underlying security. It is an estimate of how much the delta of an option changes when the price of the stock moves $1.

Gap: A gap is a break between prices on a chart that occurs when the price of a stock makes a sharp move up or down with no trading occurring in between.

GMI (signal): A series of six technical indicators developed by Dr. Eric Wish, a professor at The University of Maryland, that generates highly accurate stock market buy and sell signals.

Globalization: The tendency of investment funds and businesses to move beyond domestic and national markets to other markets around the globe, thereby increasing the interconnectedness of different markets. It has had the effect of increasing international trade and cultural exchange.

Greeks: A mathematical means of estimating the risk of stock options. Delta measures the change in the option price due to a change in the stock price, gamma measures the change in the option delta due to a change in the stock price, theta measures the change in the option price due to time passing, Vega measures the change in the option price due to volatility changing, and rho measures the change in the option price due to a change in interest rates.

Guidance: Information that a company provides as an indication or estimate of its future earnings.

Historical volatility: This is the actual price fluctuation as observed over a period of time.

Hit a Double: An exit strategy wherein an option is bought back and then resold at a higher premium in the same contract period.

Hit a Triple: An exit strategy wherein an option is bought back and resold twice in the same contract period.

Horizontal skew: The difference in implied volatility across options with different expiration dates.

Horizontal Spread: A spread (buy and sell of the same type (call or put) of option) where both options have the same strike price but different expiration dates. The terms calendar spread, horizontal spread, and time spread are interchangeable.

Hypothecation Agreement: For margin accounts, it gives the firm permission to pledge securities held on margin.

IBD 100: The Investor's Business Daily 100 is a computer-generated ranking of the leading companies trading in America. Rankings are based on a combination of each company's profit growth; IBD's Composite Rating, which includes key measures such as return on equity, sales growth and profit margins; and relative price strength in the past 12 months.

Implied Volatility: This is a forecast of the underlying stock's volatility as implied by the option's price in the marketplace.

Income statement: One of the major financial statements used by accountants and business owners. (The other major financial statements are the balance sheet, statement of cash flows, and the statement of stockholders' equity.) The income statement is also known as the profit and loss statement of operations, or statement of income.

Index fund: A type of mutual fund with a portfolio constructed to mirror, or track, the components of a market index such as the S&P 500 Index. An index mutual fund is said to provide broad market exposure, low operating expenses and low portfolio turnover. *Indexing* is a passive form of fund management that has been successful in out-performing most actively managed mutual funds.

Index option: A financial derivative that gives the holder the right, but not the obligation, to buy or sell a basket of stocks, such as the S&P 500, at an agreed-upon price and by the expiration date. An index option is similar to other options contracts, the difference being the underlying securities are indexes.

Internal rate of return: IRR is a way to analyze an investment considering the time value of money. It basically calculates the interest rate which is the equivalent of the dollar amount your investment will return.

Initial margin: The amount of a margin account as a percentage of the investment purchased on margin.

In-the-money: A term describing any option that has *intrinsic value*. A call option is in-the-money if the underlying security is higher than the strike price of the call.

Intrinsic value: For options, the amount by which the stock is in-the-money. For call options, when the underlying stock price is greater than the strike, it is the absolute value or positive difference between the stock price and the strike price. For put options, when the underlying stock price is less than the strike, it is the absolute value or positive difference between the strike price and stock price. Also, at expiration, all options must be worth zero or their intrinsic value.

Inverse ETF: An exchange-traded fund (ETF) that is constructed by using derivatives for the purpose of benefitting from the decline in the underlying benchmark.

Inverse volatility effect: Addresses the inverse relationship between market benchmark pricing and implied volatility of the benchmark (for example, the S&P 500 and the VIX).

Investor Fear Gauge: See **VIX.**

IRA: A form of an "individual retirement plan" provided by many financial institutions, that provides tax advantages for retirement savings in the United States.

Key economic indicator: Macroeconomic data that is used by investors to interpret current or future investment possibilities and judge the overall health of an economy. These are specific pieces of data released by the government and non-profit organizations. These include:

The Consumer Price Index (CPI)
Gross Domestic Product (GDP)
Unemployment statistics
The price of crude oil

Know your customer rule (KYC rule): A standard form in the investment industry that ensures investment advisors know detailed information about their clients' risk tolerance, investment knowledge and financial status.

KYC rule: See "know your customer rule"

Laddering: This is an investment technique whereby investors purchase multiple financial products with different maturity dates. I have borrowed this term and used it to describe a covered call technique where different strike prices are used for the same equity.

Lagging indicator: A technical indicator that trails the price action of an underlying asset. It is used by traders to generate transaction signals or to confirm the strength of a given trend. Since these indicators lag the price of the asset, a significant move will generally occur before the indicator is able to provide a signal. It confirms long-term trends but does not predict them.

Large cap: An abbreviation for the term *large market capitalization.* Market capitalization is calculated by multiplying the number of a company's outstanding shares by its stock price per share. The expression *large cap* is used by the investment community as an indicator of a company's size. A large cap stock has a market-capitalization dollar value of over 10 billion.

LEAPS- Long-Term Equity Anticipation Securities. These are option contracts with expiration dates longer than one year. Only the more heavily traded stocks and ETFs have these types of options associated with them.

Legging in: A way of executing a covered call trade wherein we first buy the stock and, once owned, sell the corresponding call option.

Levels of trading approval: Before you can trade options, your broker will approve you for a specific *level* of options trading. Usually, brokerages have four or five levels of approval that are based on factors such as your investing objectives, investing history and your account balance.

Leveraged ETF: An exchange-traded fund (ETF) that uses financial derivatives and debt to amplify the returns of an underlying index.

Limit Order: An order placed by a brokerage to buy or sell a specified number of shares at a specific price or better. The length of time an order remains outstanding can also be specified.

Line Chart: This is a very basic chart created by connecting a series of closing prices of a particular security with a line.

Long (position): The buying of a security, such as a stock or options contract, with the expectation that the asset will rise in value.

Long call diagonal debit spread: Constructed by taking positions on the long (buying the option) side while simultaneously taking a position on the short (selling the option) side of the market. The trade involves using different strike prices and different expiration dates and results in a net debit.

MACD (Moving average convergence divergence): A trend-following momentum indicator that shows the relationship between two moving averages of prices. The MACD is calculated by subtracting the 26-day exponential moving average (EMA) from the 12-day EMA. A 9-day EMA of the MACD, called the *signal line,* is then plotted on top of the MACD, functioning as a trigger for buy and sell signals.

MACD Histogram: A common technical indicator that illustrates the difference between the MACD and the trigger line. This difference is then plotted on a chart in the form of a histogram to make it easy for a trader to determine a specific asset's momentum.

Maintenance Margin: The minimum amount of equity that must be maintained in a margin account.

Margin account: This is a brokerage account where the client has the ability to borrow money from the broker to purchase securities. This loan is then collateralized by the cash and securities in that specific account.

Margin call: When the value of the securities in a margin account drop to a certain level, the investor will be required to put additional cash in the account or sell certain securities.

Mark: The mid-point of a bid-ask spread.

Market capitalization: The total dollar market value of all of a company's outstanding shares. It is calculated by multiplying a company's shares outstanding by the current market price of one share. The investment community uses this figure to determine a company's size, as opposed to sales or total asset figures. Also referred to as *market cap.*

Market consensus: The average earnings estimates made by brokers and security analysts. Also known as *earnings expectations.*

Market Order: An order to buy or sell a stock at the current best available price.

Market Tone: The feeling of a market (general psychology) as demonstrated by the price activity of stocks. We use the VIX and S&P 500 chart patterns to help assess this sentiment.

Marking the close: A form of market manipulation. It is an attempt to influence the closing price of a security by executing purchase or sale orders just prior to the close of trading.

Married put: When the protective put is purchased on the same day as the stock, it is referred to as a *married put* for tax purposes.

Mergers: A general term used to refer to the consolidation of companies. It is a combination of two companies to form a new company.

Mid-contract unwind: Closing both the long and short legs of a covered call trade mid-contract after maximum profits have been achieved to then use the cash to generate a second income stream.

Mini options: These are option contracts where the underlying security is 10 shares of a stock or exchange-traded fund (ETF).

This is the main difference between mini options and standard options which have 100 shares of the underlying security.

Modern portfolio theory: A portfolio optimization methodology that utilizes the mean variance of investment returns. It uses the standard deviation of all returns as a measure of risk.

Momentum indicator: Designed to track momentum in the price of a security to help identify the enthusiasm of buyers and sellers involved in the price trend development. Some indicators compare the closing price with some historical price so many periods before; others construct trend lines like the *MACD*. Others, like *Stochastics,* is a ratio using the high, low, and close values on various days.

Momentum Oscillator: A technical analysis tool that is banded between two extreme values and built with the results from a trend indicator for discovering short-term overbought or oversold conditions. As the value of the oscillator approaches the upper extreme value the asset is deemed to be overbought, and as it approaches the lower extreme it is deemed to be oversold. This oscillator is most advantageous when a stock price is in a trading range (sideways). An example is the *stochastic oscillator*

Money market securities: The securities market dealing in short-term debt and monetary instruments. These forms of debt mature in less than one year and are quite liquid. Treasury bills make up the bulk of the money market instruments. These securities are relatively risk-free.

Moneyness: Term describing the relationship between the strike price of an option and the current trading price of its underlying security. In options trading, terms such as in-the-money, out-of-the-money and at-the-money describe the moneyness of options.

Monthlys: Option contracts with monthly expiration dates, usually the third Friday of each month.

Moving average: An indicator frequently used in technical analysis showing the average value of a securities price over a set period. Moving averages are generally used to measure momentum and define areas of possible support and resistance.

Multiple Tab of the ESOC: Compare returns, upside potential, and downside protection for many stocks, all on the same page.

Nasdaq 100 index: An index composed of the 100 largest, most actively traded U.S. companies listed on the Nasdaq stock exchange. This index includes companies from a broad range of industries with the exception of those that operate in the financial industry, such as banks and investment companies.

NAV (net asset value): A mutual fund's price per share or exchange-traded fund's (ETF) per share value. In both cases, the per share dollar amount of the fund is calculated by dividing the total value of all the securities in its portfolio, less any liabilities, by the number of fund shares outstanding.

Near-the-money: Refers to options with strike prices which are near to the prevailing price of the underlying stock. The term is used often as a replacement for At-the-money options because it is rare for the share price to be exactly equal to the strike price of an option.

Net debit order: This is where you buy the stock and sell the option at the exact same time, not for specific corresponding prices but for a *limit net debit.* Also called a *buy-write*.

Net effective sale price (NESP): When selling covered call options, it is the total price of the strike price plus the option premium

Non-Standard Options: These are options that don't have the standard terms of an options contract, namely 100 shares as the underlying asset.

Odd Lot Theory: This theory is based on the assumption that the small investor is always wrong. Since these investors usually buy and sell in odd-lot amounts (less than 100 shares) and have low risk-tolerance (the theory continues), they tend to buy high and sell low. A bullish signal is when odd-lot sell orders increase relative to odd-lot buy orders.

OHLC (bar) chart: Short for *Open High, Low Close chart.* This type of chart is used to spot trends and view stock movements, particularly on a short-term basis.

One triggers other: A two-stage brokerage order wherein we enter an initial order for a stock, ETF or option, and simultaneously place a second order that's contingent upon the fill of the first order. Also known as **OTO** order.

One-time special cash dividend: A non-recurring distribution of company assets, usually in the form of cash, to shareholders. A special dividend is usually larger than standard dividend distributions.

Online Discount Broker: A stockbroker who carries out buy and sell orders online, at reduced commissions, but provides no investment advice.

Open interest- The open interest of an option contract is the number of outstanding options of that type which currently have not been closed out or exercised

Option: A contract that gives the owner the right, if exercised, to buy or sell a security or basket of securities (index) at a specific price within a specific time limit. Stock option contracts are generally for the right to buy or sell 100 shares of the underlying stock.

Option account: A brokerage account where the brokerages permit the account holder to hold options.

Option chain: A way of quoting option prices through a list of all the options for a given security. For each underlying security, the option chain tells investors the various strike prices, expiration dates, and whether they are calls or puts.

Option contract: Represents 100 shares in the underlying stock. Information included consists of the underlying security, type of option (call or put), expiration month, strike price and premium.

Option premium: The price at which the contract trades. It is the price paid by the buyer to the writer, or seller, of the option. In return the writer of the call option is obligated to deliver the underlying security to an option buyer if the call is exercised or buy the underlying security if the put is exercised. The writer keeps the premium whether or not the option is exercised.

Options Clearing Corporation: An organization that acts as both the issuer and guarantor for options and futures contracts. Also known as the **OCC**.

OTO: See "**One triggers other**"

Out-of-the-money: A call option is out-of-the-money if the strike price is greater than market value of the underlying security.

Over-the-counter option (OTC): An option traded off-exchange, as opposed to a *listed* stock option. The OTC option has a direct link between buyer and seller, has no secondary market, and has no standardization of strike prices and expiration dates. This securities market is not geographically centralized like the trading floor of the NYSE. Trading takes place through a telephone and computer network.

Overbought: A technical condition that occurs when prices are considered too high and susceptible to decline. Overbought conditions can be classified by analyzing the chart pattern or with indicators such as the Stochastic Oscillator. Generally, a security is considered overbought when the Stochastic Oscillator exceeds 80. Overbought is not the same as being *bearish*. It simply infers that the stock has risen too far too fast and might be due for a pullback.

Oversold: A technical condition that occurs when prices are considered too low and ripe for a surge. Oversold conditions can be classified by analyzing the chart pattern or with indicators such as the Stochastic Oscillator. Generally, a security is considered oversold if the Stochastic Oscillator is less than 20. Oversold is not the same as being bullish. It merely infers that the security has fallen too far too fast and may be due for a reaction rally.

Paper trade: A hypothetical trade that does not involve any monetary transactions. It is a risk-free way to learn the ins and outs of the market.

Parity: The amount by which an option is in the money. Parity refers to the option trading in unison with the stock. This also means that parity and intrinsic value are closely related. When we say that an option is *trading at parity,* we mean that the option's premium consists of only its intrinsic value.

Passive management (of mutual funds): An investment strategy that mirrors a market index and does not attempt to beat the market.

PE Ratio: P/E Ratio or Price-Earnings Ratio is a valuation ratio that compares the price of a stock to the per share earnings.

PEG Ratio: PEG = PE Ratio/Annual EPS Growth

PEGY Ratio: = PE Ratio / Expected Earnings Growth + Dividend Yield

Pinning the strike: This describes a condition with option pricing when puts and calls are near the money on expiration Friday. There is a tendency called pinning the strike for the stock to move to the strike price or slightly beyond.

Poor Man's Covered Call: This is a covered call-like strategy where a LEAPS option is purchased instead of the actual stock or ETF.

Portfolio management: The art and science of making decisions about investment mix and policy, matching investments to objectives, asset allocation, and balancing risk versus performance. *It requires organized lists of accurate information.*

Portfolio overwriting: This is where a call option is sold on a stock already part of an existing portfolio. That option is selected in a manner such that the option is NOT expected to be exercised as every effort is made to retain the equity.

Portfolio pumping: See "marking the close".

Portfolio rebalancing: Involves buying or selling assets in your portfolio to maintain your original desired level of asset allocation.

Premium report: The weekly stock screen and watch list published by the Blue Collar Investor Corp. This is a screen specific for candidates geared to writing (selling) one-month covered calls and short-term cash-secured puts.

Premium Watch List: The BCI list of screened stocks and exchange-traded funds that have passed the fundamental, technical and common-sense screens and are eligible for option-selling.

Price-to-book ratio: A valuation ratio used by investors which compares a stock's per-share price to its book value (shareholders' equity). It is an indication of how much shareholders are paying for the net assets of a company.

Price-to-earnings ratio: Ratio of a company's share price to its per share annualized earnings.

Profit and loss graph: Also called a *risk graph*, is a visual representation of the possible profit and loss of an option strategy at a given point in time

Protective collar: Conservative options collar strategy that consists of long stock, a short call, and a long put. The put is purchased to hedge the downside risk on a stock, while the short call is typically used to pay for the long put.

Protective put: A put option purchased for a stock that is already owned by the owner of the option. A *protective put* defends against a decrease in the share price of the underlying security.

Price bar: see *OHLC*.

Protective put: A put option purchased for a stock that is already owned by the owner of the option. A *protective put* defends against a decrease in the share price of the underlying security.

Put: An option contract that gives the holder the right, but not the obligation, to sell the underlying security at a specified price for a certain fixed period of time.

Put-call disparity: Deviations from put-call parity which may be used to predict future pricing.

Put-call parity: Refers to the relationship between put and call options for a given security, strike price and expiration date. Under put-call parity, the option prices should match, yielding no profit or loss.

QQQ: New ticker symbol which replaces the old QQQQ symbol for the Nasdaq 100 Trust, which is an exchange traded fund (ETF) that trades on the Nasdaq. It offers broad exposure to the tech sector by tracking the Nasdaq 100 index, which consists of the 100 largest non-financial stocks on the Nasdaq. In the past, it has been known as "cubes" or the "quadruple-Qs," but is now commonly known as the Invesco QQQ Trust or QQQ, its current ticker symbol.

Quarterlys: Options which expire on the last trading day of each quarter to coincide with end-of-quarter accounting practices. (By comparison, traditional options generally expire on the Saturday following the third Friday of the month.).

Ratio collar: Collar strategy that uses more call options than you have protective put options. The reason that you have more calls than puts (which is normally in a 1-to-1 ratio) is to provide an opportunity for higher profits if the stock rises.

Ratio valuation: The comparison of two more financial metrics located in a corporation's financial statements that reflect on the financial health of the company.

Regulation T: Also known as **Reg T**, governs the extension of credit by securities brokers and dealers in the United States. Its best-known function is the control of margin requirements for stocks bought on margin.

Resistance: The price level at which there is a large enough supply of a stock available to cause a halt in the upward trend and turn the trend down. Resistance levels indicate the price at which most investors feel that the prices will move lower.

Return on equity: Also called **ROE,** this is a profitability ratio that measures the ability of a firm to generate profits from its shareholder's investments in the company.

Reverse collar: The "Reverse Collar" is used when the investor believes that the market will be bearish. The set up would be as follows:

- A Short Stock position
- Sell a (short) Call out of the money
- Buy a (long) Put out of the money

Rho: Not considered a major Greek, measures the change in the option price due to a change in interest rates.

Risk-less collar: The investor has a risk-less collar when the net cost of the trade, or cost basis, is less than the cost of the stock alone.

Risk-reward profile: A risk reward profile is a chart of the theoretical maximum profit or loss a particular investment can have in your portfolios.

Rolling down: Closing out options at one strike price and simultaneously opening another at a lower strike price.

Rolling out (forward): Closing out of an option contract at a near-term expiration date and opening a same strike option contract at a later date.

Rolling out: Closing out of an option contract at a near-term expiration date and opening a higher strike option contract at a later date.

Rolling up: Close out options at a lower strike and open options at a higher strike.

ROI: The benefit to the investor resulting from an investment of some resource.

ROO (return on option): The percent profit realized from the sale of a covered call option based on the cost basis of the underlying stock. If an in-the-money option was sold, the intrinsic value is deducted from the option premium before calculating the return.

Rule of 72: A rule stating that in order to find the number of years required to double your money at a given interest rate; you divide the compound return into 72. The result is the approximate number of years that it will take for your investment to double.

S&P 500 (Standard and Poor's 500): An index consisting of 500 stocks chosen for market size, liquidity, and industry grouping, among other factors. It is designed to be a leading indicator of U.S. equities and is meant to reflect the risk/return characteristics of the large-cap universe.

Sarbanes-Oxley Act of 2002 (SOX): An act passed by the U.S. Congress to protect investors from the possibility of fraudulent accounting activities by corporations. It includes the establishment of a *Public Company Accounting Oversight Board* where public companies must now be registered.

Schedule D: A U.S. income tax form used by taxpayers to report their realized capital gains or losses.

Securities and Exchange Commission (SEC): A government commission, created by Congress, established to regulate the securities markets and protect investors. It also monitors the corporate takeovers in the U.S. The SEC is composed of five commissions appointed by the U.S. President and approved by the Senate. The statutes administered by the SEC are designed to promote full public disclosure and to protect the investing public against fraudulent and manipulative practices in the securities markets. Generally, most issues of securities offered in interstate commerce, through the mail or on the internet, must be registered with the SEC.

Select Sector SPDRs: Unique Exchange Traded Funds (ETFs) that divide the S&P 500 into nine index funds and managed with the objective of matching the price and yield performance of their underlying sector indexes.

Sell to open: A phrase used by many brokerages on the street to represent the opening of a short position in option transactions.

Sheltered account: A brokerage account which minimizes or decreases an investor's taxable income and, therefore, his or her tax liability.

Short (or short position): The sale (also known as *writing*) of an options contract or a stock to open a position.

Short sale: Short sale is the sale of a stock not owned by the seller. It is borrowed from the broker and eventually must be replaced. The seller anticipates a decline in equity value and realizes a profit by covering (buying back) the short sale at a lower price in the future.

Show or Fill Rule: This regulation requires the market makers to show or publish any order that improves the current bid or ask prices unless it is filled.

Short Interest Theory: This theory states that a larger short interest is the predecessor of an increase in the price of a stock.

Sideways Pattern (consolidation) – This is the horizontal price movement of an equity where the forces of supply and demand are equal. The stock simply cannot establish an uptrend or a downtrend.

Simple interest: Determined by multiplying the interest rate by the principal by the number of periods.

Simple moving average (SMA): A moving average that gives equal weight to each day's price data.

Single Tab of the ESOC: Allows you to evaluate returns from different strikes for the same stock.

Slippage: The difference between the expected price of a trade, and the price the trade actually executes at. Slippage often occurs during periods of higher volatility and when market orders are used.

Speculation: The practice of engaging in risky financial transactions in an attempt to profit from fluctuations in the market value of a stock or option.

Spin-off: Type of divestiture. Businesses wishing to streamline their operations often sell less productive or unrelated subsidiary businesses as spinoffs.

Spread: The difference between the bid and ask prices of a stock or option.

Standard Deviation*:* This is a statistical measurement that sheds light on historical volatility.

Standard Weekly options program: Standard Weeklys are listed on Thursdays and expire on the following Friday. They appear one week at a time.

Statement of cash flows: This is one of the main financial statements. (The other financial statements are the balance sheet, income statement, and statement of stockholders' equity). The cash flow statement reports the *cash* generated and used during the time interval specified.

Stochastic Oscillator: A momentum indicator that measures the price of a security relative to the high/low range over a set period of time. The indicator oscillates between 0 and 100. Readings below 20 are considered oversold. Readings above 80 are considered overbought.

Stock Scouter Rating: MSN Monet Central's rating of stocks from 1 to 10, with 10 being the best. It uses a system of advanced mathematics to determine a stock's expected risk and return.

Stock split: A change in the number of shares outstanding (in circulation). The number of shares is adjusted by the split ratio, e.g. 2 to 1. In this case, 1000 shares splits to 2000 shares but the opening price and current price are cut in half. The overall effect is to maintain the same cost and current value of an investment while increasing the number of shares and lowering the per share price. This makes it easier for small investors to own the stock in round lots.

Stop loss order: This is an order placed with your broker to sell a security when it reaches a certain price.

Stop Order: This is an order to buy or sell a security when its price surpasses a specific price called the *stop price*. At that point the stop order becomes a *market order*.

Stop Limit Order: This is a combination of a *stop order* and a *limit order*. Once activated, it becomes a limit order which means that it can only be executed at a specific price or better.

Street expectation: The average earnings estimates made by brokers and security analysts.

Strike price: The stated price per share for which the underlying security may be purchased (in the case of a call) or sold (in the case of a put) by the option holder upon exercise of the option contract.

Support: A price level at which there is sufficient demand for a stock to cause a halt in a downward trend and turn the trend up. Support levels indicate the price at which most investors feel that prices will move higher.

Technical analysis: The method of predicting future stock price movements based on observation of historical stock price movements.

Theoretical Intermarket Margining System: Also called **TIMS**, provides broker-dealers with a program which is used to compute the baseline margin requirements for Portfolio Margin accounts.

Theoretical Value: The hypothetical value of an option as calculated by a mathematical model such as the *Black-Scholes Option Pricing Model.*

Theta: Theta is an estimate of how much the theoretical value of an option declines when there is a *passage of one day* while there is no change in the stock value or volatility. Theta is expressed as a negative number since the passage of time will decrease time value.

Time decay: A term used to describe how the theoretical value of an option *erodes* or reduces with the passage of time.

Time value: The portion of the option premium that is attributable to the amount of time remaining until the expiration of the option contract. Time value is whatever value the option has in addition to its intrinsic value.

Trading range: The spread between the high and low prices traded during a period of time.

Treasury note (one of the *treasuries*): A marketable, U.S. government debt security with a fixed interest rate and a maturity between one and ten years. T-notes can be bought either directly from the U.S. Government or through a bank.

Trend analysis: An aspect of technical analysis that tries to predict the future movement of a stock based on past data. It is based on the idea that what has happened in the past gives traders an idea of what will happen in the future. The concept is that moving with trends will lead to profits for the investor.

Trigger line / signal: Usually an exponential or simple moving average of a technical indicator which serves as a frame of reference for positive and negative divergences. For example, if the MACD indicator moves above its moving average, a bullish signal is produced.

Upside potential: Additional % of profit, as it relates to the underlying stock cost basis that can be realized if the stock price reaches the strike price at expiration. It applies to out-of-the-money strike prices.

Uptrending Stock: This is a stock increasing in price with higher highs and higher lows.

Vega: Vega is the only "Greek" not represented by a real Greek letter. It is the amount that the price of an option changes compared to a 1% change in volatility.

Velocity (of money): A term used to describe the rate at which money is exchanged from one transaction to another.

Vertical skew: Refers to the situation where individual options on a particular entity have different implied volatilities that form a pattern. The pattern usually takes one of two forms: either the higher strikes have the higher implied volatilities (a forward or positive skew) or the lower strikes have the higher implied volatilities (a reverse or negative skew).

VIX- CBOE Volatility Index: Demonstrates the market's expectation of 30-day volatility. It measures market risk and is often referred to as the *investor fear gauge*.

Volatility: This is the fluctuation, not direction, of a stock price movement. It represents the deviation of day to day price changes. It measures the speed and magnitude at which the underlying equity's price changes.

Volatility skew: The difference in implied volatility (IV) between out-of-the-money, at-the-money and in-the-money options.

Volatility smiles and smirks: Common graphical shapes that results from plotting the strike price and implied volatility of a group of options with the same expiration date.

Volume: The number of trades in a security over a period of time. On a chart, volume is usually represented as a histogram (vertical bars) below the price chart. The NYSE and Nasdaq measure volume differently. For every buyer, there is a seller: 100 shares bought = 100 shares sold. The NYSE would count this as 100 shares of volume. However, the Nasdaq would count each side of the trade and as 200 shares volume.

Volume surge: An increase in the daily trading volume of an equity equal to at least 1.5 times its normal trading volume.

Wash Sale: A wash sale loss is not deductible. A wash sale occurs when you sell a stock for a loss and, within 30 days before or after the trade, buy the same stock, or substantially the same stock. This means that if you sell a stock at $35 for a loss, and buy a $35 call option, you have a wash sale and cannot deduct the loss on the stock.

Wash trading: A wash trade (not to be confused with a wash sale) is a form of stock manipulation in which an investor simultaneously sells and buys the same financial instruments.

Watch list: A list of securities that are in consideration for investment buy/ Sell decisions.

Weeklys: These are equity and index options (including ETF options) that have series that are approximately one to five weeks to expiration following their initial listing.

What Now Tab of the ESOC: Calculates the returns for a package transaction where an option is bought back and another is sold.

Whisper number: The unofficial and unpublished earnings per share (EPS) forecasts that circulate among professionals on Wall Street. They were generally reserved for the favored (wealthy) clients of a brokerage.

Wilshire 5000 Total Stock Market Index: A market capitalization-weighted index composed of more than 6700 publicly traded companies. These companies must be headquartered in the U.S. and actively traded on an American stock exchange.

Yen carry trade: A strategy in which an investor sells the Japanese currency (yen) with a relatively low interest rate and uses the funds to purchase a different currency (dollar) yielding a higher interest rate. A trader using this strategy attempts to capture the difference between the rates-which can often be substantial, depending on the amount of leverage the investor chooses to use.

Zero cost collar: Also called Costless or Zero Dollar Collar and is similar to the Riskless Collar. Essentially a Protective Collar with little or no out of pocket cost. The cost of the put is offset by the call premium. Main use is for protection of a stock position and possible unrealized capital gains

About the Author

Dr. Alan Ellman is President of The Blue Collar Investor Corp. and author of five best-selling books on the subject of covered call writing and eight books overall. His 4th book, *Stock Investing for Students,* is now required reading at The University of Maryland and 3 other universities in the US. His fifth publication, *Selling Cash-Secured Puts* is also a best-seller. He has also produced several online educational video programs on the subject of option-selling. In addition, he has written over 500 journal articles and produced over 400 videos related to stock options.

Over the past few years, Dr. Ellman, who holds a Series 65 as an Investment Advisor Rep, has been a frequent guest on financial programs such as The Options Industry Council's *Wide World of Options*. He is also a national speaker for *The Money Show* and *The Traders Expo* and has spoken at more than thirty chapters of the *American Association of Individual Investors* throughout the country. Dr. Ellman writes weekly articles for his award-winning blog as well as various financial publications in the US and abroad.

Alan is a retired dentist, a real-estate investor and a certified personal fitness trainer but dedicates the the majority of his time to educating retail investors on how to self-invest in the stock market, leveraging options, to achieve financial independence.

Barry Bergman
BCI Managing Director

Barry is Managing Director of The Blue Collar Investor Corp. and has worked with Alan Ellman for over 10 years. He produces the Weekly Premium Stock Report, develops BCI's various tools and systems, and provides ongoing coaching and mentoring services to BCI members. After graduating from engineering school, Barry began his career as a Design Engineer in the defense electronics industry. Later, he moved into high-end information technology sales and marketing, selling to the financial services industry. He has held senior management positions with both Fortune 500 companies such as Sun Microsystems and Cisco Systems, as well as early stage high tech start-up companies.

Barry began his investing career in the mid-80's trading "Telephone Switch Mutual Funds" using technical strategies. After experiencing the "Dotcom" bubble in the early 2,000's, he began an intensive educational process to learn a wide range of trading methodologies. During that process, he met Alan Ellman and has been working with him ever since.

Barry holds a BS in Mechanical Engineering from The Cooper Union School of Engineering and an MBA from the Stern School of Business at New York University. He also holds a second-degree black belt in Shotokan Karate, an Advanced Open Water Diving certification, and is a Certified Neuro-Linguistic Programming (NLP) Practitioner. Barry served in the USAF from 1968 to 1972.

Barry lives with his wife Adele in New Jersey. They have two married children, and one outstanding grandson.

www.thebluecollarinvestor.com

alan@thebluecollarinvestor.com

barry@thebluecollarinvestor.com

INDEX